THE RETREAT
FROM LIBERALISM

THE RETREAT
FROM LIBERALISM

*Collectivists versus Progressives
in the New Deal Years*

Gary Dean Best

Westport, Connecticut
London

Library of Congress Cataloging-in-Publication Data

Best, Gary Dean.
   The retreat from liberalism : collectivists versus progressives in the New Deal years /
Gary Dean Best.
      p.   cm.
   Includes bibliographical references (p.) and index.
   ISBN 0–275–94656–8 (alk. paper)
   1. United States—Politics and government—1933–1945.   2. New Deal, 1933–1939.   3.
Liberalism—United States—History—20th century.   4. Collectivism—United
States—History—20th century.   I. Title.
E806.B4944   2002
973.917—dc21   2002025329

British Library Cataloguing in Publication Data is available.

Library of Congress Catalog Card Number: 2002025329
ISBN: 0–275–94656–8

First published in 2002

Praeger Publishers, 88 Post Road West, Westport, CT 06881
An imprint of Greenwood Publishing Group, Inc.
www.praeger.com

Printed in the United States of America

The paper used in this book complies with the
Permanent Paper Standard issued by the National
Information Standards Organization (Z39.48–1984).

10   9   8   7   6   5   4   3   2   1

For my roomies,
Christina Clark and Ryan Ridgell

Contents

	Preface	xi
	Acknowledgments	xiii
	Introduction	1
1	A Leap into the Dark	11
2	Misgivings	27
3	The Combatants	41
4	Confusion in the Ranks	59
5	Creative Economics	75
6	Collectivists and the Court	91
7	Progressives and the Court	107
8	The Good Society	123
9	Disenchantment	137
	Epilogue	151
	Notes	155
	Bibliography	167
	Index	171

Preface

This book is yet another in the attempt to reexamine some of the stereotypes and conventional wisdom concerning the New Deal years that began with *Pride, Prejudice, and Politics: Roosevelt Versus Recovery, 1933–1938* (Praeger, 1990). The more I look at these years, the more I become convinced that they have been so badly botched by historians and political scientists that they are virtually a virgin field for younger scholars seeking research topics. Only political economists have so far explored the grotesqueries and follies of the New Deal in significant numbers. It is high time that historians, too, began to dig more deeply into the era.

Acknowledgments

In recent years I have received enormous and gratifying encouragement from conservative and libertarian groups and scholars, which I am happy to acknowledge here without naming them lest they be embarrassed that their support of such a curmudgeon be publicly exposed.

However, I must hereby acknowledge the assistance of one scholarly community, without whom this book might not have been written. I was able to write a first draft of it during the summer of 2000 as a result of the generous support of the Social Philosophy and Policy Center at Bowling Green State University, where I was a visiting scholar for the summer. I owe an immense debt of gratitude to everyone at the center, from the executive director, Fred D. Miller, Jr., deputy director, Ellen Frankel Paul, and associate director, Jeffrey Paul, to the hardworking secretaries and research assistants who went out of their way to accommodate my needs. I thank you and all of those who contribute financially to the success of the center from the bottom of my heart.

I must also thank the staff of the University of Hawaii at Hilo library, particularly its former director, Kenneth Herrick, for their unfailing assistance, and a succession of student helpers that included Chelsea Keehne, Mary Jane Badua, and Christina Clark.

Introduction

In the modes of their thinking, the intellectuals who expound
what now passes for "liberalism," "progressivism," or "radicalism," are almost all collectivists in their conception of the
economy, authoritarians in their conception of the state, totalitarians in their conception of society.
                    Walter Lippmann, *The Good Society*, 1937

That a crisis occurred for American liberalism in the 1930s is generally accepted. Conventional wisdom has it that Franklin Delano
Roosevelt resolved that crisis by redefining liberalism to meet the
demands of the situation, carrying liberalism to its apotheosis or its
culmination, thereby saving capitalism. That Roosevelt contributed
to the redefinition of liberalism by his acts and policies is not at question. A liberal tradition, however, had always existed in American
political culture, albeit under different names. Most recently, it has
been described as progressivism during the first decades of the
twentieth century. Measured against that liberal tradition, the acts
and policies of Roosevelt's New Deal created important crises for
American liberalism that are not well understood.

In his valuable work, *Encore for Reform*, Otis Graham has described the dilemma faced by those progressives who had battled for liberal causes earlier in the century when they confronted the collectivist liberalism of the New Deal under President Franklin Delano Roosevelt. For some, the New Deal seemed a delayed opportunity to at last achieve many of the goals for which they had striven nearly two decades earlier, and they embraced both its goals and methods. For many others, however, the methods and/or the goals of the New Deal seemed inconsistent with the earlier progressivism, or at the very least highly suspect, and their positions ranged from criticism to opposition. In limiting his work to their response to the New Deal, however, Graham omitted their reaction to the broader currents of liberalism in the 1930s, of which the New Deal was only a part.

It is commonplace to give Franklin Delano Roosevelt and the New Deal undue attention, I think, for the shift in American liberalism in the 1930s. James Young, for example, writes that Roosevelt "redefined the basic ideological vocabulary through which Americans conducted politics."[1] It is certainly true that FDR redefined the Democratic Party during his presidency, but the shift in the definition of liberalism should, instead, be ascribed to the Great Depression, and Roosevelt's was only a part in the drama.

The redefinition of liberalism had begun well before Roosevelt's inauguration in the pages of the leading liberal magazines—*The Nation* and *The New Republic* (*TNR*). Traditional American liberalism, which called for the preservation of the capitalistic system, properly regulated by government to prevent monopoly and other abuses, had been abandoned by those journals before March 1933. The new liberalism was anticapitalist and collectivist, and it made common cause with socialists and communists in a sort of liberal common front against the capitalist enemy. Traditional liberals put their emphasis on the resumption of industrial production as the way out of the depression, while the new liberals of the 1930s were convinced that productive capacity had outstripped the nation's ability to consume under capitalism, and that a new collectivist economic order must be constructed in which the emphasis would be on a more equitable distribution of goods rather than on increased production. The Brandeisians, as represented by the views of David Cushman Coyle, fell somewhere between these two extremes.

The antagonism to capitalism on the part of the collectivist liberals stemmed primarily from one of two motives, both born in the apparent failure of capitalism in the 1930s. The first was the belief that capitalism was dead, a proven failure, and that it should be replaced by a collectivist system. The second, based as much on the

European experience as the American one, viewed capitalism as a positive danger, in that it had apparently served as a springboard to fascism in Italy and Germany. That eventuality could be headed off in America only by the creation of a collectivist system. Bruce Bliven and *The New Republic* can be identified with the former position, Freda Kirchwey and *The Nation* with the latter.

As Young points out, Louis Hartz missed the originality of liberalism during the New Deal years. Hartz, like so many historians, had a tendency to pour the waters of New Deal-era liberalism into old, familiar jars—like Jefferson and Hamilton in the early republic, the New Nationalism of Theodore Roosevelt and the New Freedom of Wilson during the progressive era, and the wartime mobilization during World War I. But the New Deal, Young observes, had "a social democratic [that is, collectivist] cast, which had been missing from earlier reform efforts." Young, however, fails to note that the New Deal's social democracy was but a pale shadow of the social democratic liberalism that gripped many reformers in the 1930s, and many of the examples he gives of New Deal social democratic legislation were, in fact, more in the traditional progressive mode than social democratic.[2]

One of the most influential collectivist voices among liberals in the 1930s was that of Harold J. Laski, British Marxist and Labour Party official, who welcomed the advent of what he saw as capitalism in a stage of historical crisis. Capable of seducing the public so long as it provided prosperity, its collapse in the 1930s had brought the class struggle to the fore. Laski found attempts to reform the economy along traditional liberal lines to be unrealistic, therefore, and called for radical changes in the social order along Marxist lines. Echoing Laski, the editors of *The New Republic* concluded their discussion of the Supreme Court decision invalidating the National Recovery Act (NRA) in 1935 with the following statement: "Either the nation must put up with the confusions and miseries of an essentially unregulated capitalism, or it must prepare to supersede capitalism with socialism. There is no longer a feasible middle course."[3]

Despite Laski's friendship with Roosevelt and his frequent trips to the White House, it is difficult to accept Young's view that FDR tried "to reconstruct the Democratic Party along the lines of a European social democratic party."[4] What Roosevelt did, instead, was to try to reconstruct the party into one that would follow him blindly wherever he led in his pursuit for greater personal power, and it was this reality, even more than his policies, that horrified traditional progressives. As Thomas Corcoran would later recall, Roosevelt was "a genius in the accumulation and exercise of power."[5] Corcoran observed further: "Somewhere along the line Roosevelt came to believe—or acted as if he believed—that the President was endowed with unspecified powers 'to promote the general welfare'. . . . [H]e chose to interpret that high-sounding clause in the Preamble like his cousin Theodore would, to mean that a man of his vision (and unprecedented popularity) could use whatever tools came to hand or to mind for the nation's benefit."[6]

There was, in short, a Rousseauvian cast to the Roosevelt years that has not received enough attention, one that revealed itself both in a Rousseauvian emphasis on egalitarianism and in the concept of a "popular will" expressing itself through a strong leader. It was a concept encouraged in Roosevelt's mind by Laski and by Felix Frankfurter.

Most revealing, a French admirer of Laski wrote in 1930 that Laski had "a profound knowledge not only of the psychology of the French Revolution but of the great prerevolutionary thinkers, notably Rousseau."[7] Indeed, his views and his advice to Roosevelt seem filled with a Rousseauvian emotionalism and egalitarianism, a kind of mystical belief that a union was being achieved between the will of the American people and their supreme law-giver, a union so powerful that it could and should ignore all restraints in its path, whether they be legislative, judicial, constitutional, or federalist. And perhaps Laski's major contribution to the turmoil of 1930s American liberalism was the corrosive effect of this belief on Roosevelt and many of his supporters during the New Deal years.

Collectivists faced a dilemma in the 1930s. On the one hand, the economic collapse and attendant distress had discredited the old order and seemed to offer the prospect for radical change. On the other, no amount of wishful thinking could disguise the fact that the American people had ignored the collectivist parties in 1932 and elected a candidate running on a decidedly conservative Democratic Party platform. Contra the old, or traditional, left's position that the creation of a socialist state must precede comprehensive planning, however, the new collectivists were convinced that the Great Depression offered a rationale for inaugurating some innocent, semingly innocuous ventures into planning that could serve like the camel's nose in the tent. Before the capitalists knew it, the entire socialist camel would be inside displacing them. The National Industrial Recovery Act (NIRA) and Agricultural Adjustment Act (AAA) were the noses of the collectivist camel. As one *The Nation* editor put it after six months of the New Deal, "This is Roosevelt's role—to keep the people convinced that the state capitalism now being set up is entirely democratic and constitutional."[8]

In their attempt to coexist planning with the democratic system, however, collectivists faced the same problem that Herbert Croly had grappled with a quarter-century earlier in *The Promise of*

American Life—how to resolve economic planning from above with democratic politics from below.[9] They hit upon the same solution that Croly apparently had—rule by a leader so popular that he could carry the masses with him wherever he chose to lead. Croly thought he had found such a leader in Theodore Roosevelt; the new collectivists looked to his cousin Franklin. Thus the simultaneous efforts to imbue FDR's willing mind with his role as personification of the will of the masses, to gain for him large electoral majorities by whatever means necessary, to expand his powers as president, and to shape the Democratic Party in his image.

Young accurately observes the following:

There were basic shifts of power not only away from the states and toward Washington but also within the central government as legislative supremacy gave way to a system of presidential government. This shift was accompanied . . . by huge delegations of power from Congress, which was presumably setting basic standards of policy, to administrative agencies, which were presumably filling the mere details left by the legislation. But . . . it became clear that the agencies were making coercive decisions of their own.[10]

In fact, the legislation sent to Congress from the White House and obediently enacted into law by the legislators was purposely drafted in such ambiguous fashion that it granted them virtually a blank check to define both their powers and methods. Written for the most part by young disciples of Louis Brandeis and Felix Frankurter, the legislation reflected their profound distrust of banking and big business, their disillusionment with the ability of Congress to deal with them, and their seizure of this opportunity to transfer the law-making powers from Capitol Hill to the hands of agencies that were, themselves, largely staffed with their disciples. It symbolized a transition away from government by laws and to the arbitrary rule by men. Such a trend could hardly be described as liberal, nor those who instigated and supported it as liberals.

In fact, the entire concept of government advocated by the collectivist liberals could scarcely have been more at odds with the liberal tradition in America or with the Constitution. Impatient with all restraints on their power, whether from the states, Congress, or the courts, they considered, as economist Isaac Lippincott put it, "their power as personal property to be used in the manner that their reasons and whims decide." As Rexford Tugwell explained it, the sole function of Congress was to transfer "wide emergency powers" to the White House, whereupon the traditional function of Congress would be carried out by a cabal of nonelected and inexperienced advisors in deciding the specific policies to be followed. Thus, the Congress elected by the people was not regarded as a partner in government, nor even as part of a system of checks and balances, but as a rubber stamp on policies formulated without public debate by the White House junta. As Lippincott put it, "Thereby was ushered in a period of laws framed in secret council, of star-chamber conferences, of innumerable measures forced upon a docile Congress, and of drastic penalties attached to control measures. . . . Herein democracy in America sank to the lowest level in history." And the conventional wisdom is that this marked the apotheosis of liberalism![11] According to Edmund Wilson, Tugwell had said during the hundred days that America was getting "Fascist economics without a Fascism movement," and that with the passage of the AAA his "job would be done."[12]

But in retrospect, even Thomas Corcoran was less than enthusiastic about the trend he and his fellow New Dealers had inaugurated, writing the following in his unpublished autobiography: "The fundamental issue was whether Congress, addressing economic problems of a new magnitude could confer new powers to the executive agencies; the old Supreme Court said 'no.' When attrition brought new intellectual blood to bear, the Court changed its institutional mind. . . . But today the burdens of administrative law arising from the creation of those prerogatives alone threaten to overwhelm the Federal court system."[13]

As Theodore J. Lowi has pointed out, under Roosevelt the federal government was adopting two entirely new kinds of functions, new at least for the federal government of the United States.

These functions were *regulation* and *redistribution*. In adopting a large number of regulatory policies, the federal government had discovered that there was national as well as state police power. As for redistribution, conventional labels refer to fiscal and monetary policies, but these bland labels mask the true significance and the novelty for the federal government of the redistributive function.

Although regulatory and redistributive policies are quite different from each other, they share one very important characteristic which also distinguishes . . . them from almost everything the federal government was doing prior to the 1930s: These two new functions involved the federal government in direct and coercive use of power over citizens. Washington policy-makers could no longer hide from themselves the fact that *policy* and *police* had common roots.

These additions of function were accompanied by equally fundamental changes in institutional relationships and in public philosophy. . . . In any event, it was during the New Deal that we began the . . . change from a Congress-centered government to an executive-centered government. That development is in turn highly correlated, in cause and effect, to another commonplace feature of the New Deal, the rise of *delegated* power. The federal government literally grew by delegation. Although Congress continued to possess the lawmaking authority, it delegated that authority increasingly in statute after statute to an agency in the Executive Branch or to the president, who had the power to subdelegate to an agency. . . . Ultimately, delegation was recognized for what it really was—administrative legislation.[14]

Frankfurter's interests went beyond merely the increased federal control of bankers and businessmen that was the program of the Brandeisians. Ekirch finds that Frankfurter stressed the "profoundly important psychological factor of a growing disbelief in the fairness of our capitalistic scheme," and urged Bruce Bliven, editor of *The New Republic*, to publish articles that exposed the selfishness and dishonesty of high officials. Although he admitted that the fault was with "the system," Frankfurter argued

One of the basic aspects of "the system" is the authority wielded by "big men"—the geocentric position accorded to the successful business men and financiers. Nothing, I believe, sustains the present system more than the pervasive worship of Success and the touching faith we have in financial and business messiahs. Therefore it is that I believe it to be profoundly important to undermine that faith. . . . Undermine confidence in their greatness and you have gone a long way towards removing some basic obstructions to the exploration of economic and social problems. *You* don't have to worry about "what next?"

"You cannot reconstruct the whole of society at one fell swoop," Frankfurter warned Bliven, "and you and I will be in our graves before there is a planned society in this country. But you can do a great deal towards it by dealing with the concrete issues that carry your general philosophy forward."[15]

Nothing could be more revealing of Frankfurter's deviation from the views of Louis Brandeis, for whom a planned economy was anathema. Some time earlier Frankfurter wrote to George Soule, Bliven's coeditor at TNR, in a similar vein that

It is an essential of democracy that we have responsible government. Ministries in business and finance, as in political government, should fall when they make miserable failures. Our kings of finance and captains of industry are all in office. They are still allowed special authority and men still listen to them. Commanders-in-chief—generals or admirals—who bring such disasters upon their country, or fail to avert them, are court-martialed. Similar treatment should be meted out to the Mellons and the Millses, the Schwabs and the Mitchells, the Tom Lamonts and the Insulls and all their ilk.[16]

From this and numerous other evidence it is clear that the foremost Brandeisian had deserted the liberal views of Brandeis by the 1930s, largely under the influence of the Harold Laski, and had joined the forces of the enemy—the collectivist liberals of the Tugwell, Bliven, Soule, and Laski stamp. One finds little recognition of this in Frankfurter biographies, but when the great divide came between the two camps, Frankfurter stood with Brandeis's enemies. That great divide was Roosevelt's effort to reshape the Supreme Court in 1937. The motive of the collectivists in encouraging and supporting the move was clear and undisguised—to eliminate the one obstacle in the way of a return to the collectivist economic planning of the first New Deal. Frankfurter's support for the action revealed where his sympathies had been all along, squarely in the camp of the collectivists.

It is well known that primarily three schools of economic thought contended for influence in the early New Deal. There were the planners, identified with Rexford Tugwell, avowed collectivist, as well as Raymond Moley, Adolf Berle, and others who had been influenced by the theorists of Theodore Roosevelt's New Nationalism. They were largely responsible for the National Industrial Recovery Act and the Agricultural Adjustment Act. There were also the Brandeisians, whose hand was seen in some aspects of the NIRA, but more notably in the securities legislation of 1933 and 1934. Finally, there were the inflationists, whose influence was visible in the departure from the gold standard, the Thomas Amendment to the AAA, and the gold-buying debacle of late 1933.[17]

Their influence having been relatively brief, and too minor to rival the drama of the war between the planners and the Brandeisians, the inflationists have received little attention from historians of the New Deal. Viewed in the context of the larger ideological debate of the 1930s, however, the inflationists, who put their emphasis on recovery from the depression through one variety or another of inflation, deserve more attention. The ranks of traditional progressives and liberals were largely made up of inflationists, and it was the failure of the New Deal to emphasize their strategy for producing recovery that caused so many of them to initially experience the disenchantment with FDR and the New Deal that Otis Graham described.

In an even larger context, Roosevelt's failure to embrace the inflationary solution of the traditional progressives, and to instead simultaneously straddle the contrary programs of the planners and Brandeisians, led the New Deal up a series of antibusiness blind alleys and dead-end streets that not only delayed recovery, but also prevented the adoption of the comprehensive program of genuinely liberal reform that veteran liberals sought, thus leaving the nation with a liberal legacy based on arbitrary rule and subsidies siphoned from the public treasury.

The war between the planners and the Brandeisians went largely to the former until Brandeis, himself, took a hand in sinking their NIRA flagship by joining in the 9–0 Supreme Court decision against it in the Schechter case in early 1935. After the decision, Brandeis lectured his New Deal disciples that it had changed "everything. The President has been living in a fool's paradise."[18] There now ensued what some historians have labeled the "second New Deal," one in which they identify Brandeisian ideas as most influential. Early New Deal brain trusters like Tugwell and Moley found much of the second New Deal alien to their emphasis on planning of the economy. However, Brandeisianism had ceased to seem so anachronistic by this time, largely because of the contribution of engineer-turned-economist David Cushman Coyle in fitting it into a more comprehensive and cogent framework.[19]

Nevertheless, as Ekirch points out, while the new direction was "more conventional in its progressivism, and accepting the concept of regulation in lieu of the positive planning and control favored by a Tugwell or a Richberg, the Second New Deal was nevertheless radical in its aid to labor and small farmers and in its broadened program of federal unemployment relief."[20] It also demonstrated innovative new ways to use the taxing power that was so central to Brandeisian thought, even in ways that could be turned to the objectives of the planners.

But while the more moderate of the planners, like Moley, abandoned the fray, the die-hard collectivists among them, like Tugwell, Frankfurter, and Laski did not. Feeding Roosevelt's considerable vanity and pride, and his well-known prejudices, they framed the issue in terms of business and finance as the enemy, with the court as accomplice, and counseled defiance and confrontation. In 1936 the court struck down the AAA, and a year later FDR went on the offensive with his bill to "pack" the court. It meant that the war between the collectivists and the Brandeisians had broadened and intensified, had, in fact, moved onto Brandeis's own turf.

Few besides the collectivists were aware of the real stakes. When the bill was defeated, most of its opponents viewed it as a defeat for FDR's dictatorial ambitions, and historians even today debate whether FDR lost the battle, but won the war with the Supreme Court, when in fact the president was only a tool in a larger struggle. The real losers were the collectivists, including Brandeis's erstwhile disciple Felix Frankfurter. And they lost again in Roosevelt's failed attempt to purge the Senate of some of his opponents in the 1938 primary elections.

Among those who opposed the bill could be counted many veteran liberals, including some, like Senator Burton K. Wheeler, who had until that point generally supported the New Deal. While the defection of these latter appeared sudden, the court bill seems only to have been the match put to the fuse of their accruing doubts about FDR and the New Deal. For others, like Amos Pinchot and Senator Hiram Johnson, the issue only confirmed their long-held and expressed opposition to the president. These two had supported FDR in the 1932 election and for varying periods afterward, until forced by his policies to choose between collectivism and traditional liberalism. The private anguish over those policies expressed in Hiram Johnson's letters to his sons probably typifies that of many other veteran liberals to whose thoughts we are not privy.

The subsidization of America under the New Deal for the sake of the leader's political fortunes obscured the loss of liberty that was taking place under it. With so many Americans dependent on the federal government for one subsidy or another, Maurice Hallgren wrote, the New Deal had "enormously accelerated the movement toward centralization and regimentation in every field of political and economic endeavor. To a degree unprecedented in the republic's history farmers, workers, bankers, manufacturers, and others were told by their government precisely what they could and could not do." That these federal subsidies and their accompanying dictates were in some ways beneficial did not alter "the fact that all of them encroached upon individual liberty." Yet, Americans voiced little criticism, as if united in a code of silence lest their own form of federal spigot be turned off.[21]

This work will attempt to describe the changes and conflicts taking place in liberalism during the 1930s by examining principally eight individuals who were representative of both proponents and opponents of the shifts taking place. Bruce Bliven and Freda Kirchwey edited the two most respected liberal journals during these years, *The New Republic* and *The Nation*, and their views represent those of the journals they edited. Behind much of the new direction that American liberalism was taking stood another figure, Harold Laski, a British Marxist, who might be termed the *eminence grise* of collectivist liberals. More traditional liberalism and its reactions to the changes taking place are represented by Amos Pinchot, Hiram Johnson, Felix Morley, and Walter Lippmann. Another approach, closer to that of traditional Brandeisian liberalism, is represented by engineer-turned-economist David Cushman Coyle. Into this mix, in lesser degrees, will be added other influences on the liberalism of the 1930s.

— 1 —

A Leap into the Dark

Bruce Bliven was an unlikely prospect to become a leading collectivist liberal in the 1930s. His early life, in fact, closely paralleled that of an ideological opposite, Herbert Hoover, in that both were born and raised in small Iowa towns and graduated from Stanford University in California. But whereas Hoover pursued a career in mining, Bliven was early drawn to journalism. It was while with *The New Republic* from 1923–1955 that Bliven exerted his greatest influence, particularly during the 1930s. His newspaper experience had introduced him to a number of the radicals, reformers, and muckrakers of the progressive era, including "Big Bill" Haywood of World War I and Lincoln Steffens. Bliven's move to *The New Republic* was a natural, and when its founder and general editor, Herbert Croly, suffered a paralytic stroke in 1928, Bliven succeeded him as general manager.

There were many linchpins that guided Bliven's collectivist views. Two were Felix Frankfurter and Harold Laski, both of whom Bliven met in the early 1920s and with whom he maintained contact through the 1930s. Frankfurter, he wrote, seldom let a week go by without "at least one communication from him, frequently handwritten, praising or attacking things we had published, suggesting topics for articles, and, in many cases, nominating possible writers."[1] Laski, whom Bliven described as "one of the most brilliant talkers and writers of his generation," wrote for *TNR* in the 1920s, and continued to do so, but less often in the 1930s.[2] After Herbert Croly's death in 1930, Bliven and George Soule took on joint responsibility for the magazine, with Bliven handling the major editorial responsibilities.

Bliven and *The New Republic* welcomed the inauguration of the New Deal in March 1933. In a 1951 oral history interview, Bliven recalled that *The New Republic* had, in fact, been for the New Deal long before Roosevelt embraced it. The original members of FDR's brain trust, the Columbia University group that included Rexford Tugwell, Raymond Moley, and Adolf Berle, were New York City friends of *The New Republic* staff while Roosevelt was still governor of the state.[3] An indication of that closeness, and of the collectivist views of *TNR* as early as January 1932, can be seen in a letter from coeditor George Soule to Rexford Tugwell soliciting an article. Soule wrote, "it would be in the nature of a reply to those on the Left who argue that there is no use talking about planning before we establish Socialist or Communist rule. You could argue that if we began to plan at all, as we must, we should have a bear by the tail and could not let go, until at some time in the future we should find that we had set up a Socialist economy. That would be the end of the process and not the beginning."[4]

In short, the beginnings of planning in a capitalist economy would be like the camel's nose in the tent, with capitalists awakening one morning to find that the whole socialist camel was inside.

Tugwell did, in fact, begin to take this point of view in his writings. In a paper published as a supplement to the *American Economic Review* two months later, Tugwell noted that a number of businessmen, including Henry I. Harriman, head of the U.S. Chamber of Commerce, and Gerard Swope of General Electric, had already naively advocated voluntary planning of the nation's economy, and Tugwell wrote

Strange as it may seem—directly antithetical to the interests of business and unlikely to be allowed freedom of speech, or say nothing of action—it seems altogether likely that we shall set up, and soon, such a consultative body. . . . It seems to me quite possible to argue that, in spite of its innocuous nature, the day on which it comes into existence will be a dangerous one for business. . . . There may be a long and lingering death, but it must be regarded as inevitable.

The superiority of rational planning to the chaos of capitalism would soon become apparent, and business would "logically be required to disappear. This is not an overstatement for the sake of emphasis; it is literally meant."[5]

Once the New Deal was fully underway, by contrast with the conservative platform on which FDR had been elected, *The New Republic* became one of its most devoted supporters. Dedicated, like the early brain trust members, to the concepts of economic planning and federal regulation of the economy, Bliven gained a reputation as an "intellectual godfather of the New Deal," although he frequently criticized the Roosevelt administration for not going far enough in the desired directions.

TNR was as popular with the New Dealers as the New Deal was with *TNR*. Visitors to Washington offices commented on the magazine's prominence atop the desks of New Deal functionaries. And the depression was good to *TNR*. Circulation climbed by two-and-a-half times during the 1930s, from 12,000 to nearly 30,000.[6] Late in life, Bliven recalled for an interviewer that even a magazine of limited circulation could exert a "tremendous influence" if read by "the leaders in the community." He explained, "In the case of *The New Republic*, when I was the editor, we were read by the editors of the daily papers all over the country. When we would launch an idea in our pages, I would see it coming back in the editorials from dozens of newspapers in big towns and little towns everywhere. So you can spread ideas remarkably well that way."[7]

Well before Roosevelt's election, Bliven had written of Americans that in their "volatility, intensity, violence of thought and action and mercurial changeability," their temperament was "much more Latin than Nordic."[8] Clearly, by 1932 that volatility was manifesting itself in wide-scale criticism, even repudiation, of values that Americans had held dear until the 1930s. The profit motive and capitalism were excoriated from the pulpit no less than by radicals, and the popularity and prestige of businessmen and bankers plummeted to the point that they became the butts of cruel jokes. New Dealer Thomas Corcoran recalled that Americans had blamed the depression on Wall Street "bogeymen," and were "chanting for their blood."[9]

Clearly a sea change was underway, at least temporarily, in the views of even everyday Americans, and the opportunity seemed to lay open for sweeping changes in the nation's social, political, and economic life while it lasted. Yet Max Ascoli found in it all a common strain with the speculative frenzy of the 1920s, writing the following:

Only a nation of gamblers would conceive and afford the New Deal. A revolution without alternatives, a record-breaking leap into the dark, this is something that could be undertaken only by a people accustomed to stockmarket speculation in the grand manner. The Roosevelt administration is attempting a kind of socialization of the gambling mentality; the stake is the creation of a new system for the distribution of opportunities among the American people. This aim is pressed forward in the old glorious way of a nation of poker players. It is the great gamble to end gambling. Perhaps, if the experiment succeeds, the people who pass through this great trial will have strengthened their individual sense of self-reliance and will valiantly gamble again; if the experiment fails, the people will gamble as much as they ever did.[10]

It was a prospect that electrified demagogues of both left and right during the 1930s. In an editorial, *TNR* opined: "People are seeking a Messiah, some mystic and powerful savior who will put everything right."[11]

Less than a month after Roosevelt's inauguration an unusual movie was released with considerable ballyhoo in one hundred cities across the nation. The movie was unique in the history of American film, for the final version bore the imprint of two sitting American presidents and of one of the most powerful publishers in the nation. The movie was *Gabriel Over the White House*. It was based on an English book, published in the United States under the same title—a book that Herbert Hoover later described as "Roosevelt's 'Mein Kampf.'"[12]

When Roosevelt entered the White House the nation had been in the grip of three years of economic depression. Impatient with sterile debate instead of action, many Americans revealed a desire for results with little regard to the niceties of means employed. The mood of the nation was ripe for an assertion of strong executive leadership after months of legislative paralysis. Typical of the mood was publisher Barnarr McFadden, who wrote in June 1932, "What we need now is martial law; there is not time for civil law. The President should have dictatorial powers."[13] Even the noted liberal columnist Walter Lippmann had argued that Congress should defer to presidential leadership and that power should be concentrated in his hands. Felix Frankfurter, noted liberal law professor at Harvard University, was sufficiently discomfitted by such sentiments that he wrote Lippmann shortly before FDR's inauguration to say that he was "troubled" by the "general impression" Lippmann had given "that Congress is an awful nuisance, and that that Jack-in-the-Box ought to be shut up. It ought all to be left to the Great White Father." The positions of the two men would before very long be reversed over the issue.

Gabriel Over the White House unabashedly advocated a presidential dictatorship for America. The movie reflected the popular demand in America for action, helped to prepare Americans for Roosevelt's assertion of leadership, and may well have exerted a considerable influence on the Roosevelt White House. In the book, in particular, a number of bills were passed that bore an uncanny resemblance to Roosevelt's subsequent program, including one that provided for "packing" the Supreme Court. Others included a $5 billion bond issue for enhancing consumer spending (which at the same time provided the president with funds to "buy" the obedience of the states), the creation of a National Reconstruction Corps organized along military lines to undertake public works projects, and a Department of "Education" to sell the administration and its programs to the American people. It also provided for inflation and mortgage-debt relief.

As Roosevelt would rely on his "fireside chats" over the radio for the same purpose, the president in *Gabriel* won over public opinion by direct weekly appeals over television. The movie president was disdainful of the press, observing to a reporter that "when it comes to influencing public opinion, I'll do that with sight and sound." One of his supporters observed that "publicity and advertising have been the mediums by which almost every great leader has established his hold on the people."[14]

Anticipating Roosevelt's own view of the Constitution, the fictional president told a TV audience that none of the great presidents of American history, not even "Washington or Lincoln or Wilson...would permit a mere document, no matter how sacred, to bind the hands and shackle the rights of their own people, struggling mightily with grievous adversity in another age and under completely changed conditions." When told that he is proposing dictatorship, the fictional president replies that he is "a believer in democracy, but democracy requires leaders."[15]

The movie president was, wrote one reviewer of the book, a "benevolent Social Fascist," "an enlightened Mussolini," who ignored "the machinery of democracy" and state and local authority to push through his policies of inflation and "soak the rich" taxation.[16] It was, another wrote, the story of "a President who overrode the Constitution, the Supreme Court and Congress and ran things with a high hand."[17] Curiously enough, while dismissing the likelihood of such a scenario in America, few reviewers found the course of action outlined in the book to be unrealistic.

The book reached the screen largely through the influence of media tycoon William Randolph Hearst, who embraced it as a propaganda vehicle for issues dear to his heart. Hearst was at this time supporting Roosevelt for the presidency, and one of his biographers concludes that the movie was a kind of "celluloid letter" from the publisher to the president he had helped to elect a few weeks earlier, in which he outlined desirable policies and methods for Roosevelt to follow.[18] It was, columnist Walter Lippmann observed, "a dramatization of Mr. Hearst's editorials."[19]

Apparently the movie was screened at least twice in the Roosevelt White House before its release, and alterations were made in it before Roosevelt adjudged it as containing "nothing objectionable." On 1 April 1933, Roosevelt wrote Hearst to tell him "how pleased I am with the changes which you made in *Gabriel Over the White House*. I think it is an intensely interesting picture and should do much to help."[20] Meanwhile, in late March and through much of April, the Hearst newspapers carried a serialized version of the Gabriel story that was a curious blend of the book and the film. The emphasis on dictatorial powers in both was retained, the packing of the Supreme Court was omitted from both the movie and the serialization.

Hearst spared no efforts in promoting the movie through his newspapers. One large advertisement shrieked "Dictator in the White House" in bold print. The bally-hoo no doubt contributed to the movie's success at the box office. *Gabriel* was one of the six most popular films in April 1933, as measured by ticket sales.

Roosevelt's involvement in, and approval of, a movie that unabashedly supported a presidential dictatorship over the United States must be deemed surprising at the very least. This was, one film historian has observed, no fantasy tale, but rather a "totally credible" design for the "Americanization of dictatorship." Another wrote that the movie "evolved its President out of a tradition as straightfaced and reverent as a grammar school history lesson. . . . An American fuhrer would be like the guy next door, and in a time of crisis no one would notice the Bill of Rights being shredded to bits."[21] It was, yet another reviewer noted, "almost, but not quite beyond the realms of possibility."[22]

Predictably, American liberals attacked the movie. For *The Nation*'s reviewer, the "all-too-evident purpose" of the film was "to convert innocent American movie audiences to a policy of fascist dictatorship in this country."[23] Bruce Bliven reviewed the movie himself for *TNR* and agreed that it was "a half-hearted plea for Fascism," and "a very naive piece of Hearstian wish-fulfillment." Audiences, he predicted would be "as enthusiastic over the abandonment of democracy" as over the "reverential mouthings about Lincoln."[24] One wonders what these two liberal journals might have said had they known of FDR's editing and approval of the film before its release.

Hearst's promotion of, and the liberal reaction to, *Gabriel* are interesting in light of what was to follow. Under the impact of FDR's

New Deal, Hearst would move into opposition and rail against the very same tendencies toward centralization of power in the White House that he had advocated in the movie. Bliven and his fellow collectivists at *TNR* and *The Nation* would convert to support of the same centralization, including FDR's 1937 attempt to pack the Supreme Court, that they had decried in their reviews. Nothing could better illustrate the degradation into which liberalism was passing in the 1930s than the alteration of views concerning the issues raised in *Gabriel*.

The new breed of collectivist liberal was convinced that it was part of a great historical event—the passing of an old era and the dawn of a new one. The end result would be revolutionary change, but they differed somewhat over whether it should be achieved at revolutionary or evolutionary speed. Bliven quoted the views of a kindred soul in Washington who told him "Two things to remember. First, that what is now being done can never be undone. If the New Deal succeeds we can't go back; if it fails, we can't—no matter who wants to or how much. The command is forward, from now on, and the movement is certainly toward the left."[25]

But for Bliven and *TNR* the early New Deal seemed to be putting far too much emphasis on recovery from the depression, and allowing the historic opportunity for major reconstruction of the system to dribble away. At best, the much ballyhooed National Recovery Administration (NRA) was an ineffectual band-aid when major surgery was required; at worst, under a leader like Hugh Johnson, it smacked of a crude fascism in which the rights of the consumer and worker were subordinated to the interests of big corporations.[26]

Bliven and *TNR* leaped, however, to the defense of those aspects of the New Deal they favored. In mid-1933, Bliven wrote Frankfurter of a concern in Washington among New Dealers, including some of the Brandeis disciples, that Wall Street was jeopardizing passage of the Securities Act by threatening "to sabotage it by simply not issuing any new securities," and that presidential adviser James Warburg was trying to get FDR to shelve the measure. Bliven wondered if it might not be advisable for *TNR* to enter the fray.[27]

Like many of the new breed of collectivist liberals, Bliven and *TNR* early embraced the theories of John Maynard Keynes. But Roosevelt, himself, seemed still so under the spell of orthodox economic views as to the merits of budget balancing and the dangers of large deficits, that he was resistant to the massive deficit spending that Keynes believed necessary to stimulate recovery and provide employment. Keynes's open letter to the president, and his conferences with FDR in Washington in 1934, suggested that perhaps Roosevelt would now be converted to the Englishman's theories, but it did not happen.

In December 1934, Harold Laski and John Maynard Keynes debated the question: "Can America Spend Its Way Into Recovery?" in an unlikely site—*Redbook* magazine. The Laski position is revealing of the mixed feelings collectivists harbored concerning Keynes's proposal for recovery. For Keynes, the answer was so obviously yes that "No one of common sense could doubt it unless his mind had first been muddled by a 'sound' financier or an 'orthodox' economist." It was, in fact, "impossible to suppose that we can stimulate production and employment by *refraining* from spending." He explained:

The rest of the community is enriched by an individual's expenditure—for his expenditure is simply an addition to everyone else's income. If everybody spends more freely, everybody is richer and nobody is poorer. . . . To refrain from spending at a time of depression, not only fails, from the national point of view, to add to wealth—it is profligate: it means waste of available man-power, and waste of available machine-power, quite apart from the human misery for which it is responsible.

And when the individuals of a nation were unwilling or unable to spend at an adequate level, "it is for the government, the collective representative of all the individuals in the nation, to fill the gap." Deficit spending, of course, put the nation into debt, "But the debt of a nation to its own citizens is a very different thing from the debt of a private individual. The nation is the citizens who comprise it— no more and no less—and to owe money to them is not very different from owing money to one's self." Moreover, he wrote, the alleviation of unemployment "as a result of government expenditure, means a considerable reduction in outgoings on the support of the unemployed. At the same time the receipts from taxation mount up as the nation's taxable income increases, and as real property values are reestablished." The whole purpose, however, was to stimulate private spending. Specifically, Keynes advocated a program of governmental guarantees to stimulate housing construction, in this way encouraging a maximum of private spending by a minimum of expense to the government. But "even pure relief expenditure is much better than nothing. The object must be to raise the total expenditure to a figure which is high enough to push the vast machine of American industry into renewed motion."

Laski, however, warned the deficits thus produced must be paid eventually from taxation, which would mean "increased costs to manufacturers of goods," increased prices, and a reduction in the volume of demand, which would only result in unemployment once again. Laski went on:

Unless, therefore, recovery of a normal kind rapidly supervenes, the consequence is . . . the need for a system of controls (of wages, the price of materials, profits, etc.) of the kind known during the war. It is, of course, impossible to limit these controls to a narrow field of industry. The more government operations continue, the wider must be the range of its interference. The logical result . . . is to end the workability of the assumptions upon which the traditional capitalist system depends.

Laski concluded that "government spending as anything more than a temporary and limited expedient will necessarily do harm in a capitalist society." A small dose of such spending did no harm, but "the prolongation of the dose ultimately means a movement to a planned society in which the control of capital and labor is determined by the state." Such a society, he wrote, would be "incompatible with the principles of capitalism," and could only end in a "planned society . . . based on the public ownership of the means of production." Desirable as Laski considered that, he pointed out that it was not the avowed goal of the New Deal.[28] While desirable as a device for alleviating unemployment, then, the best outcome for collectivists lay in it not producing recovery.

For those who were already disillusioned with capitalism, or at least with capitalists, events in Europe provided new arguments against it. The apparent support of capitalists in Germany and Italy for dictatorial regimes committed to saving capitalism from communism turned old arguments that democracy and capitalism were synonymous into cruel jokes. Instead, it now appeared that when capitalism faced a crisis, as it clearly did in the 1930s, it could serve as a stage in the direction of a fascist dictatorship. That it had happened in Europe seemed proof that it could also happen in the United States. Thus, even for those who did not believe that capitalism was dead, the hastening of its death was fervently to be wished in order to prevent a repetition of the German and Italian experience in the United States. It also encouraged those of such views to look kindly upon the Soviet Union and to regard socialists and communists in their midst as allies against domestic fascism.

For Freda Kirchwey, editor of *The Nation*, capitalism must be replaced by "some form of widespread social control or ownership and social planning."[29] Only in this way could the prospect of fascism be averted in the United States. She was encouraged by the inauguration of Roosevelt, particularly by his apparent willingness to act in behalf of the unemployed and others suffering from the depression, and because he had surrounded himself with "idea men" whose thinking *The Nation* found congenial to its own. Kirchwey and *The Nation* now sought to add that journal's voice to those around the president in urging him to act boldly. *The Nation* wrote: "The life of the country is at low ebb. Mr. Roosevelt need not fear to try new leaders and new ideas, and to venture boldly into untrodden paths."[30]

But when Roosevelt embarked upon the "hundred days" he showed no apparent disposition to eliminate capitalism, only to reform it and to submit it to greater government control. His programs Kirchwey dismissed as diversions, rather than as answers to the fundamental questions that were besetting society. There were some positive benefits in the National Industrial Recovery Act, but its apparent emphasis on shoring up capitalism and stimulating a temporary recovery did not go to those fundamental issues. "She wanted," her biographer writes, "the federal government to take over the banking, transportation and communication industries, thereby removing private profit and giving labor a fair share of wealth," but she recognized that Roosevelt had no such mandate from the voters. Nevertheless, *The Nation* opined in June that Roosevelt "could have and should have moved farther to the left."[31] By the end of 1933, Kirchwey could acknowledge that the president had shown a commitment to "prosperity based on social control and a wider distribution of social benefits," even if that commitment had not yet produced much in the way of results.[32]

By early 1935 the collectivist disposition of *The Nation* had become offensive to some traditional liberals, like Amos Pinchot, who wrote Kirchwey to complain that the magazine "had gone clean away from liberalism into communism. That, of course, is your business, though it seems pretty silly to me." He was sorry, he told her, because he was "rather fond of The Nation. And I'm also fond of liberalism, which I think has far more power to do something useful and fundamental in this country than has the communist philosophy."[33] When Kirchwey denied his charge, Pinchot responded that "its content, its emphasis, and choice of subject, would warrant the assertion that it is, on the whole, rather a communist publication."[34]

Like many veteran progressives–liberals, Pinchot was devoted primarily to one solution for the deflation and unemployment of the depression. Months before Roosevelt's inauguration, Pinchot described himself as "a fairly convinced inflationist, or reflationist," and he was encouraged that "almost every economist I know is abandoning his old sound dollar citadel and becoming at least open-minded on the subject." But Pinchot also supported deficit spending for public works and considered that it might be desirable to reduce the length of the working day to achieve "a fair balance between the number of jobs available and the number of men seeking jobs." The objective of all government policy should be the restoration of "adequate purchasing power for the masses." Pinchot was initially confident that Roosevelt would pursue policies similar to those he advocated.[35]

If inflation were not resorted to, Pinchot warned, the nation would emerge eventually from the depression with "its money and credit concentrated to an incredible extent in a few peoples' hands," which meant also that power would be concentrated in those same hands, and the nation would subsist only "on such terms as we can obtain from a master class."[36]

Pinchot campaigned for Roosevelt as a member of "Progressives for Roosevelt," and was pleased with the new president's cabinet choices, especially that of his old friend and fellow progressive, Harold Ickes, as Secretary of the Interior. Pinchot's attitude toward the new administration was "enthusiastic, hopeful—yet not overconfident." He welcomed Roosevelt's farm and reforestation programs, but neither they nor the saving of the banks would "go very far toward reducing the debt structure, putting people back to work, or getting purchasing power into the pockets of the masses," such as inflation would accomplish. While the New Deal policies had instilled a certain amount of confidence in the nation, Pinchot did not consider the problems confronting Roosevelt to be psychological. They were due rather "to the country's purchasing power being today in the hands of people who don't have to spend money on consumption." Again, he advocated deficit spending on public works, such as he and others had urged unsuccessfully on Hoover in 1930. It might, he admitted, "load the future with perplexities," but "I don't see the masses buying commodities from the shops. I don't see the shops increasing their orders to the wholesalers, or the wholesalers buying from the factories, or the factories going to the banks and showing statements that warrant loans, until buying is started up in a big way with dollars from the pockets of the masses." If Roosevelt did not act decisively and soon, "his so-called dictatorial powers will fade away as Congress begins to assert its independence and asks (after patronage day is over) for its relinquished powers of which it is so jealous."[37]

In early April 1933, Pinchot wrote an article for *Polity* advocating an "out and out inflationary or reflationary policy." Citing John Maynard Keynes, Pinchot argued that the deflation of the depression must be met by "an inflationary movement of equal power" to "restore the balance, and redistribute purchasing power." While the president had "worked a miracle or so," if he did not embrace "a policy of controlled inflation" he would "have to go the way of Hoover." But Pinchot despaired that "the deflationists seem to have the ball at Washington just now."[38] A few weeks later, however, Pinchot was cheered when Roosevelt took the United States off the gold standard. It was at least "a step in the right direction," and he praised the president for "his refreshing ability to do things without all kinds of inhibitions and prejudices getting in his path. He seems to be as direct as a child and very shrewd too."[39]

As noted, Pinchot had already become concerned over the swirl of new influences within traditional American liberalism. He wrote an editor of *Polity* that the journal should be "a magazine frankly defending capitalism, with all its drawbacks, as the best economic system devised so far," but also advocating the reforms that were necessary to make it work efficiently and fairly. He thought such a magazine "would have an immediate appeal . . . to lots of people who are sick of the communist drivel, and who don't believe in socialism or think it's practicable in the U.S.A."[40]

Looking at the concentration of power in Roosevelt's hands, over which some were already voicing concern, Pinchot wrote that he was not as "grieved by the substitution of wartime for democratic form of government as I thought I should be." He did not think "the death and burial of democracy," some were decrying was serious because "our dictatorship has a string to it," although he admitted "that this is the way everybody talks when dictatorship comes around." He liked, he said, "the open-mindedness" of Roosevelt's administration, although some might call it "lack of principle. But it certainly has the advantage of being lacking of prejudice too." FDR's "rapid-fire program, week after week, is one of the most remarkable political feats in modern history. The man's spiritual and mental energy is astounding, and wholly admirable." Roosevelt was "not only breaking down the psychology of depression, but the depression itself," although Pinchot was still convinced that recovery could only come through "a redistribution of wealth as a means of restoring the buying power of the masses." Still, he considered Roosevelt's "attack on the depression is real, though it doesn't embody our program." The president reminded him "of a cowboy I saw in Montana, driving a big tin can across the prairie, with two revolvers which he discharged alternately with his right and left hand."[41]

After six months of the New Deal, however, Pinchot's letters began to reflect a growing uneasiness over the powers being concentrated in the White House. Noting that the NRA closely resembled the system in fascist Italy, Gilson Gardner wrote Pinchot that he was "frightened at the thought that we are paddling along in the path of the biggest dictator."[42] Pinchot admitted that he was, himself, "appalled by the magnitude of the changes that are being made, and by the amassing of power in the hands of a single individual, a policy which, though necessary no doubt, in an emergency like the present one, is full of terrific dangers. What I hope is that Roosevelt will dissolve the dictatorship at the right moment."[43]

He hoped, Pinchot wrote another liberal, that Roosevelt would be "a big enough man to realize the disadvantages of getting the country into the 'trust the President' state of mind."[44] But while admitting that he did not "wholly believe in the philosophy behind the New Deal, except as an emergency philosophy," Pinchot was convinced that with "twelve million people out of work, something must be done, whether it jibes with one's pre-conceptions or not."[45]

Despite the concentration of power in the White House, however, recovery was not taking place. Pinchot was more than ever convinced that "currency inflation, cleverly managed," was the only method for bringing about the necessary redistribution of income and increase of purchasing power. The NIRA and AAA, on the contrary, had reduced purchasing power by raising prices more rapidly than wages. He wrote publisher Roy Howard that if Roosevelt delayed inflation much longer it would be "his first great blunder in timing, and jeopardize not only the public's, but his own welfare."[46] As prices continued to rise without corresponding increases in incomes, the president's popularity must inevitably have suffered.

Still, Pinchot remained defensive of the man he had supported for the White House, writing a year after the election

My personal opinion of the Roosevelt administration is that it is trying to make, and perhaps succeeding in making, reforms that are absolutely necessary to the continuance of capitalism. Professors or no professors, it seems to me the program is on the whole an intelligent and needful one. And I think that if it's given a chance, it will get very good results. We must remember that we are in an emergency which, perforce, drives the administration to measures which in ordinary times would be out of place.[47]

But the failure of the NIRA and AAA to produce recovery led Pinchot to advocate currency inflation with greater urgency. In April 1934, he wrote directly to Roosevelt to say that "when governments, corporations, or individuals are oppressed by an unbearable burden of debt, there is only one sensible solution. It is to cut the debt down—repudiation is really what it amounts to—by inflation."[48] And two months later he added that "the country requires a real inflation (I mean more *new* money and a very great deal of it in the public's hands) before the debtors, federal, state and local government, as well as private debtors, can stagger out from under the fixed obligations and price levels rise, with new buying."[49]

When Roosevelt still did not act, Pinchot wrote the pro-New Deal publisher of the *New York Post* that it was "time to attack the President for his failure, not merely to do what he promised about restoring the normal sized dollar and the price level, but for making no sincere determined effort to do those things, to the accomplishment of which he solemnly pledged his administration." FDR needed to be told "that he cannot get away with a sop-to-everybody policy that leaves the public in the lurch." It was clear to Pinchot that the New Dealers could not, themselves, grasp the complexity of the "kaleidoscope" that they had created, and "which they are constantly trying to patch up by contradictory and often silly experiments." Reflecting his growing disenchantment with the New Deal, Pinchot went on:

For an administration to create, acknowledge, and confine itself to a bounded and understandable program, no matter what it may be, is one thing. For it to change its ground from day to day, inventing stopgap measures to compensate for failures, and leaving everybody who employs labor in a state of uncertainty and fear, which renders it impossible to make commitments, start up industry and hire people, is quite another thing. . . . Mr. Roosevelt's program seems to me to have grown into a patchwork of unrelated parts. It could not possibly be put over except through an extended dictatorship, and not then, I believe.[50]

When the People's League for Economic Security, of which he was a member, put out a leaflet that Pinchot objected to, he wrote its author, Dr. Henry Pratt Fairchild that the organization had to "fish or cut bait. Be for capitalism or against it." For himself, Pinchot was opposed to socialism or communism as impractical for America and probably everywhere else. There was a role for the league only "if it devotes itself to an attempt to destroy any privilege and injustice and perversion that have grown up within capitalism, and give a cleaned-up capitalism a trying out on a better basis. That has been the liberal position right along, and I think the sound one." The more he saw of collectivists, Pinchot wrote, "including those in the government, the more I feel convinced that the future of the country depends upon an opposition that stands for capitalism, private property and the profit system against socialism, communism, and fascism, and works for a minimum program of reform such as we have drafted."[51]

After weeks of debating with Fairchild through letters over the relative merits of capitalism versus socialism, Pinchot severed his connection with the People's League for Economic Security, writing the professor that socialism could only succeed to the accompaniment of "an amount of regimentation and loss of liberty and choice that will be worse even than what we have experienced under the impaired form of capitalism we have known since the Industrial Revolution." Capitalism, Pinchot insisted, was "the main essential of human development; that the last thing we want in our brief span is a regimented life."[52]

Pinchot's opposition to regimentation would no longer be confined to the sterile debates with Dr. Fairchild. Early in March 1935, he wrote to pro-New Deal Senator Peter Norbeck that, while he agreed that Congress had been wise in centralizing power in the White House "for the time being," he felt "that time is now over. And the power Congress has given away should be got back somehow, so that you men on the Hill can control the New Deal's I think disastrous attempts at regimentation."[53]

— 2 —

Misgivings

Felix Morley was the brother of the better-known writer Christopher Morley, whose major distinction was winning a Pulitzer Prize as editor of the *Washington Post* in 1936. A self-described liberal, Morley had not, like many traditional liberals, been a Bull Moose Progressive with Theodore Roosevelt in 1912, but had instead been an admirer of Woodrow Wilson's reform presidency. When he assumed the editorship of the *Washington Post* in December 1933, after its purchase by Eugene Meyer, Morley was determined to make it the newspaper of choice among the Washington elite, and to this end he sought to steer the newspaper along a middle-of-the-road path—to be "both impartial and dynamic," as he put it—that eschewed the more conservative views of Meyer and his wife—an objective that was not always easy of attainment.[1] Insofar as the *Post*'s editorials were critical of Roosevelt and the New Deal, the negative tone stemmed less from Meyer's conservatism than from Morley's concern over the administration's abandonment of traditional liberalism.

Morley began to keep a journal on 5 March 1934, the first anniversary of the New Deal, in which he recorded his growing misgivings about FDR and his administration. In that initial entry, Morley wrote, "Across the boards men and measures tread a strange fandango. The decay of the old order proceeds. But signs that anything is being prepared to take its place are none too assuring."[2]

On 21 March, Morley editorialized in the Post about the administration-sponsored Bankhead Bill, writing that, while it regimented only cotton farmers, the "trend toward a centralized dictatorship in agriculture is unmistakable." Similar bills for other commodities were already before Congress or being considered. The government's control over agriculture was "being broadened as well as intensified," and some officials were worrying that a Pandora's box had been opened.[3]

When the William Wirt story broke later in the month, wherein the Gary, Indiana school superintendent reported overhearing a conversation by several young New Dealers in which they allegedly described the revolution they were carrying out in Washington, and labeled Roosevelt their Kerensky, Morley downplayed the revolutionary aspect of the story, but found Wirt's charges significant nevertheless, writing in a *Post* editorial that it had helped "to concentrate widespread attention on the fact that much current legislation has implications, and would institute changes, going far beyond the immediate evils at which it seems to be directed." Wirt's charges had only spotlighted the fact "that a number of measures sponsored by the Administration have no connection with economic recovery, and are far more likely to protract the depression than to shorten its course."[4]

A few days later, Morley returned to the episode, writing of the New Deal's "group of rather inexperienced enthusiasts who, drunk with unaccustomed authority, seem to think they have a monopoly on all political and economic wisdom." It was ridiculous to call them communists, but their "egoism, conceits and overbearing self-righteousness" made them dangerous. They were, he wrote, "incredible young playboys who regard the United States as their private laboratory for untested social and economic experimentation."[5] Typical of their errors, Morley found, was their belief in the efficacy of laying high taxes on the well-to-do, a practice that not only caused revenue to shrink but also delayed recovery. Penalty taxes on industry would not benefit those who were employed by those same industries.[6]

When the American Bar Association issued a report recommending a number of changes in the Securities Act of 1933, Morley editorialized that the lawyers were "in an ideal position to view the operation of the Securities Act objectively." The New Deal's reaction to their proposed amendments would be a test of the administration's commitment to recovery. If undermining of the present economic system was the goal of the Roosevelt administration, then the Securities Act was the perfect instrument, since it would "force the Government to take over the business of providing capital." If that was not the objective, then the private investment market would have to be assisted through the amendment of the law .[7]

The *Post* then sent out telegrams to a large sampling of industrial and financial leaders to ascertain their feelings on the effects of the law in stifling investment and recovery, and the replies overwhelmingly faulted the law for paralyzing the financing of industry.[8] Surveying the results, Morley editorialized insightfully that a sharp "cleavage" was being drawn between those who supported necessary reforms, and those in the administration who seemed determined to create "atrophy of business enterprise." Unless the New Deal chose "to see business recovery halted," it could not afford to ignore any longer the testimony of those being crippled by the law.[9] But Morley had earlier editorialized that "So far the planning has been by those whose work indicates that they would view with satisfaction the destruction of existing institutions," although it was "scarcely to be believed that the Administration is knowingly endorsing such purposes."[10]

Morley appraised the year-old legacy of the hundred days in an April editorial, writing that Congress had begun to "take stock" of the emergency legislation passed during the "legislative reign of terror" of the hundred days. In its haste to pass whatever the White House sent to it, without due consideration or debate, Congress had consented to what was, in effect, "the rule of a dictator," and had brought discredit upon itself, even as European legislatures had paved the way for dictatorships by similarly allowing their powers to be usurped.[11]

When Roosevelt expressed opposition to the general revision of the Securities Act of 1933, which was widely considered to be an obstacle to recovery, Morley editorialized that minor "tinkering" with the law would serve no purpose. Uncertainties about its meaning needed to be clarified, "ill-defined liabilities and unfair penalties" needed to be removed. The measure should be clarified to remove uncertainties as to its meaning. Ill-defined liabilities and unfair penalties, applicable to issuing companies and their directors as well as to underwriters must be eliminated, "unreasonable rules and regulations together with onerous registration requirements ought to be abrogated."[12]

Two months later he recorded in his journal his opposition to the Wagner Labor Bill, which sought, in his view, "to do through the dictatorial agency of the State what can only be safely accomplished through the cooperative action of industry itself." He added, "The way in which many of my radical friends welcome a progressive growth of Etatism [statism] which can only lead to some sort of Fascism continues to perplex me."[13]

In May 1934, Morley was invited to address the Institute of Public Affairs at the University of Georgia, where he told his audience that the New Deal was bringing some substantial advances in domestic policy, notably in "the abolition of child labor through the NRA codes, the development of a national employment system, the movement for the establishment of unemployment insurance, and the better organization of industry" also through NRA codes, but the negatives outweighed the positives. On the negative side, Morley decried "the growth of bureaucracy, the centralization of authority at the expense of state and local governments, and the extension of political influence into new forms of state enterprise," which posed dangers to America's traditional system of government. Morley explained, "Limitation of individual enterprise, whether on the farm, in business, or through labor policies, and regimentation of the American people" threatened the success of the New Deal.[14]

A few days later he bemoaned

the purely emotional radicalism which is about today, and which if uncontrolled can of course only end by bringing us to dictatorial forms of government which must ceaselessly stimulate the aroused passions of the mob in order to retain control. Since these passions can always be most easily directed against the foreigner we slip paradoxically from radicalism to an inflamed nationalism destructive of most of the aims—liberty, peace, cooperation—for which the emotionalist believes he stands.

On the contrary, Morley admired "the cool, detached, liberal yet nonemotional type of mind," of which he saw so little in Washington.[15]

As Congress prepared to adjourn two weeks later, Morley noted that the national debt was now $400 million above the World War I peak it had reached in 1919, but that Roosevelt seemed unconcerned about it. He added: "All except the more stupid or sentimental of Roosevelt supporters seem now to realize that he is without any consistent or reasoned political philosophy. But his humanitarianism, plus Federal largesse, are so far carrying him through." Morley suspected, though, that the president "has moments now when he feels highly disquieted at the failure of any fundamental pick-up."[16]

In mid-July, Morley opined that "the truly serious troubles of the Administration do not come from either Right or Left, but from its own superficiality & lack of political principles. Pleasant moralization alone will not see us through." Yet there was as yet no alternative to the New Deal. It was, Morley wrote, "amusing to watch the Republicans, conscious both of their opportunity & their un-popularity, trying to give birth to a political philosophy. It will take a Caesarian to get it out of most of their accredited leaders!"[17] After lunching with two Republicans a few days later, Morley added that they admitted "the old Bull Moose [progressive] leadership . . . is scattered from Hell to Breakfast, & what G.O.P. leadership will be without that element neither of them like to admit."[18] The "Bull Moose leadership" referred to, included, of course, such Republican "irregulars" as Senators George Norris of Nebraska, Hiram Johnson of California, William Borah of Idaho, and Robert LaFollette of Wisconsin, as well as nonoffice-holders like Amos Pinchot, many of whom had supported FDR in 1932 under the banner of "Progressives for Roosevelt."

Late in July 1934, Morley addressed the failure of the United States to recover under the New Deal. There was, he wrote, a "grow-ing fear that the Administration may have gone so far into the se-ductive maze of squander-mania as to be unable to retrace its steps," rather than providing "normally functioning investment markets, which in turn depend upon stable money and adequate protection of creditor interests." Morley explained that the New Deal over-whelmingly favored debtors at the expense of creditors, the effect of which would be to destroy the will to save and invest, thus leav-ing monetary inflation as the only alternative to provide needed funds.[19]

The working of what Max Lerner would later refer to as the "dia-lectical processes" in Walter Lippmann's thought during the course of the collectivist liberalism of the New Deal years is almost pain-ful to survey. Particularly striking is the abuse to which he was exposed by those who rightly regarded him, in the context of the times, as a "conservative liberal," but who were unable or unwill-ing to submit their own "liberalism" to the self-examination that characterized Lippmann's. Collectivist liberals like Bruce Bliven, Felix Frankfurter, and Harold Laski, were contemptuous of what they regarded as his liberal pretensions, arguing that his associa-tion with the Republican *New York Herald-Tribune* and his Wall Street connections had converted him into a defender of the status quo, more interested in his elevated position than in the concerns of genuine liberals. George Soule, coeditor of *TNR*, thought "some-one ought to do a study of him as a sample of the kind of liberal whom the radicals rightly distrust," as if distrust by radicals were somehow a badge of disgrace.[20] Even Amos Pinchot teed off on Lippmann in articles in *The Nation* in July and August 1933, and was rewarded with praise from a number of the new breed of col-lectivist liberals. Felix Frankfurter wrote Pinchot that he had performed "a notable public service" by divesting " a "false god" of liberalism, of its "meretricious authority." Pinchot's essays had, he said, stripped Lippmann of "the appearance of disinterested and liberal scholarship" and proved that Lippmann was "not a scholar in his reporting of the social—economic scene and is quite lacking in that disinterestedness which is his moral panacea."[21] Approving letters also came from Oswald Garrison Villard, Harold Ickes, and others.

Max Ascoli wrote of such "intellectuals" as Frankfurter, Bliven, and colleagues that they had "a pathetic desire to escape the puritanical rules of pragmatic philosophy, such as loyalty to the inductive system, fanaticism for so-called facts, the birth control of ideas; and they relish in the Marxian philosophy the voluptuousness of the a priori, the deliberately partisan interpretation of reality, the monogamy with one idea, or at least with one scheme. And they can reach such thrilling heights as to declare Mr. Justice Brandeis a reactionary and the period of reforms gone forever."[22]

It is well known that Lippmann's opinion of FDR the candidate was distinctly negative, yet he embraced the new president with considerable enthusiasm as a result of Roosevelt's decisive handling of the banking crisis and other early actions of the administration. During the hundred days, Lippmann muted his criticism of the Agricultural Adjustment Act and the National Industrial Recovery Act, but it was clear that, in common with other veteran liberals like Pinchot, he preferred a controlled inflation that would promote recovery without recourse to such unprecedented devices as the AAA and the NIRA. And while other syndicated columnists like Mark Sullivan and Frank Kent worried over the concentration of power in the White House that resulted from the passage of these and other early New Deal acts, Lippmann accepted them at face value, as emergency legislation that would not become permanent agencies or powers.

In describing the beneficial results that flowed from inflation, Lippmann explained that it made it expensive to hoard money, forcing people to spend their money and causing prices to rise, which in turn led them to spend more, causing prices to rise anew. Thus an inflationary spiral was set in motion to reverse the deflationary spiral of the depression. By contrast, maintenance of the gold standard created "the intolerable strain of falling prices," and pushed the Roosevelt administration "further and further toward schemes like the farm bill, the thirty-hour bill, and these latest proposals for 'mobilizing' industry, all of them hopelessly intricate devices to counteract the effect of a general fall in prices." Such a program of "controlled inflation" as he advocated would not produce instant recovery, Lippmann acknowledged, but it would "stop the economic rot and permit us to recover," and it would serve as an alternative to the regimentation contemplated in such New Deal proposals as the AAA and NIRA.

The rising economic indices of the summer of 1933 were proof for Lippmann that recovery was underway. Ignoring the influence that fear of higher prices was playing in the "upturn," as businessmen and investors embarked on a frenzy of buying in anticipation of the impact that inflation, the NIRA, and the AAA would soon exert, Lippmann was confident that the foolish aspects of the New Deal were not hampering recovery. Although the president had been granted powers that, if used, could cause great damage, he saw no evidence that Roosevelt was "afflicted with delusions of grandeur," or "that he is plotting against the Constitution." When the economy sagged later in the summer, coincidental with the inauguration of the NIRA and the AAA, Lippmann, like Pinchot, again called for a managed inflation that would rekindle the lagging recovery momentum.

While he considered much of the New Deal to be misguided and lacking coherence, Lippmann recognized that the public expected Roosevelt not only to produce recovery, but also to "respond to the conviction of the mass of the people that the old order of things up to 1929 needs drastic renovation." This necessity to pursue recovery and reform policies simultaneously must inevitably complicate the efforts in both directions and make recovery more difficult than if there were a singleminded devotion to recovery alone. Not only was there a conflict between programs, but within programs as well. The NRA was a case in point. The recovery contributions of that agency Lippmann found retarded by its reform objectives. Desirable as those reform objectives might be, Lippmann clearly did not believe that they should be allowed to interfere with recovery.[23]

By his emphasis on recovery over reform, Lippmann separated himself from the collectivist liberals who clearly preferred reform. It was not simply a matter of priorities. For traditional liberals like Lippmann and Pinchot, an early recovery would eliminate the billions required annually to succor the unemployed and would mute, if not silence, the demands for collectivist reforms that they considered inappropriate for America. For the collectivist liberals, recovery was unimportant so long as the unemployed were cared for by the federal government, particularly since they could be safely counted upon to vote for "Santa Claus." They had no great objections to a weak and discredited business and finance, wishing only that it should become even weaker and more discredited, thus opening the door to further reforms. While they paid lip service to recovery, the conditions they imposed for one made it very unlikely that a recovery could occur.

Although he was clearly uncomfortable with the mixture of policies and programs that went under the New Deal heading, and was impatient with the lack of concentration on recovery, Lippmann showed little concern for the issues being raised by fellow journalists Mark Sullivan, Frank Kent, and David Lawrence. When Sullivan charged that the vast array of powers given to the president smacked of fascism, Lippmann responded that the analogy was wrong because the authority of the president was not sustained by a private army, as in fascist Italy, nor was there any censorship of the press, nor any imprisonment of political opponents. Roosevelt was not governing by force, but by the popularity his results so far had achieved. After a year of the New Deal, Lippmann wrote, "A careful and objective examination of the measures taken in this past year, and of the way the executive powers have actually been exercised will show, I believe, that the social philosophy of the New Deal is in spirit, in objective, and in method wholly alien to Fascism and Communism." Where the administration's policies were concerned, it was "not conspiracy that we have to worry about. It is confusion."[24]

Even those within the New Deal were well aware of the rapidly shifting kaleidoscope. Corcoran and Cohen wrote Frankfurter in mid-1934, as the law professor was about to return to the United States from a sojourn in England, to try to acquaint him with the changes he would find. They told Frankfurter, "Much has gone over the dam since you went away and affairs have proceeded pretty far toward concrete forks in the road. The Tugwell crowd has been pushed by its enemies—and its own loose talk—away over to the left. Ray [Moley] is vacillating considerably toward the right. Isaiah [Brandeis] is militant and impatient in the middle. You'll need, we should think, considerable detailed knowledge of what has gone on just to listen understandingly."

With Moley's help, they had arranged a meeting between Brandeis and FDR that had ranged over various issues, most especially the forthcoming social security legislation. They also suggested that Frankfurter try to make up relations between Moley and Jerome Frank. Moley, they told Frankfurter, was "really important and you're going to find yourself strangely straddled between Isaiah on one side who wants to ride ahead hard with his full program, completely contemptuous of political obstacles—and Ray on the other side, who is afraid of Isaiah's belligerence, quite through with the agony and sweat of reforming, and wearily eager to settle down to a false security of sweet reasonableness." Jerome Frank, they said, was eager to have Frankfurter as "an ally because he fully realizes the inherent weakness of his and Rex's position."[25]

Roosevelt's actions in 1935 were deeply distressing for Lippmann as they were for many other Americans. One of these actions was the president's initial attempt to push through Congress his "soak the rich" tax bill without allowing normal procedures for study, debate, and possible revision of the legislation. Roosevelt's leadership had degenerated into "a distracted, episodic turning hither and thither," that seemed obsessed over "remote and minor issues." The crisis of the early New Deal years had passed, but Roosevelt gave no indication that he realized it. His attempt to push his 1935 legislative package through Congress "without hearing or debate," indicated that he was still acting now "as if it were the dark winter of 1933." It all led Lippmann to question his earlier confidence that Roosevelt would relinquish the emergency powers he had been granted once the emergency were over. Instead, he now worried that Roosevelt was abusing "the extraordinary powers intrusted to the President for meeting an emergency." He did not mean, he assured his readers, to imply that Roosevelt had "the ambitions of a dictator," but he worried that the president had "let zeal, political calculation, the intoxication of power, heat and fatigue, confuse his grasp of a very simple, but very fundamental principle," namely the need for "such a thing as due process, not merely in law, but in morals and in democratic methods."[26]

Roosevelt's state of the union speech of January 1936 was disquieting to many traditional liberals, both for its contents and for the circumstances of its delivery. Delivered before Congress at 9 P.M., the trappings resulted, as the *Washington Post* put it, in Roosevelt using "Congress as Hitler uses the Reichstag, as a sounding board from which he can exalt himself and denounce all opposition." Lippmann agreed that "never before has the radio been used in America with such calculated purpose to establish any one man's domination of public opinion."[27] As usual Lippmann put forth the disclaimer that he did not "believe or wish to imply that Mr. Roosevelt has any intention of abusing the propagandist procedure which he has invented," but he worried that the president had set a precedent for "those who could very easily abuse it, and . . . the spectacle . . . is one which should not pass unchallenged as a precedent for the future."[28]

Privately, however, Lippmann wrote that he was "becoming increasingly troubled about the Roosevelt administration," and had "begun to feel that a situation might develop as a result of a kind of loss of balance where it would be absolutely necessary not to re-elect Mr. Roosevelt." He was worried that the strains of the presidency had "produced effects which raise serious doubts as to whether he can remain master of the situation which he is creating."[29]

That the content of Roosevelt's speech was less disturbing for Lippmann than the mode of delivery probably resulted from the fact that the president had not revealed in it anything of which Lippmann wasn't already aware and concerned. For some, however, the warnings of Sullivan, Kent, Lawrence and others about the growth of presidential powers had fallen on deaf ears until Roosevelt made an issue of it himself in the speech. His administration had created "new instruments of public power" in the past thirty-four months, he admitted, which were entirely "wholesome and proper" if exerted by "a people's government," like his, but which could be dangerous if allowed to fall into the "the hands of political puppets of an economic autocracy" and to be used to "provide shackles for the liberties of the people." The implication was that Roosevelt had amassed power in the presidency that only he could be trusted to use wisely and justly.[30]

The Democratic Omaha *World Herald*, which had consistently supported Roosevelt and sneered at charges that he was gathering too much power in his hands, was stunned by the speech. For weeks it raked that portion of FDR's speech on its editorial page, writing three weeks after it was delivered, "The purpose of our democracy, from the beginning, has been to shackle government so it would be powerless to shackle the people, in whatever hands power might temporarily be reposed. The thought that deliberately it should be made possible for any administration, the best or the worst, to shackle liberty is repellant. Mr. Roosevelt, when he made the quoted statement, laid himself wide open to the attack of his opponents, both liberals and conservatives."[31] From similar qualms, the Democratic St. Louis *Post-Dispatch* would join the *World Herald* in opposing Roosevelt's reelection in 1936.

One bit of emergency legislation that seemed to Lippmann likely to become permanent was the emergency expenditures for relief and to other interest groups like agriculture. As Lippmann put it, "Once these obligations become permanent, the Congressmen who are likely to be elected are the Congressmen who have pledged themselves to increase the appropriations." Such a situation presented "a grave danger not only to the finances of the government but to the moral habits of the nation." Roosevelt, he wrote, had committed himself to "two main lines of policy which he is unable to carry out and is unable to abandon." One of these was the "collectivist measures which the Supreme Court has invalidated." The other was "the distribution of Federal funds in great amounts to large groups in the population." Of the former, Lippmann wrote that it was unfortunate for Roosevelt "to hold a philosophy of social reconstruction which he cannot reconcile with the constitutional system under which he lives," and yet he was "evidently determined not to renounce his personal philosophy." Lippmann was appalled by Roosevelt's apparent indifference to the fact that temporary relief was rapidly turning into permanent subsidies. What was happening, he wrote, was that "large groups throughout the country . . . are becoming accustomed to receiving money which appears to be available without costing the mass of the people anything. It is an illusion." It had created "great vested interests among large groups of voters" that was "an appallingly dangerous thing." Such a system of "permanent bounties to large groups of voters is one of the surest and commonest symptoms of the decay of democratic societies."[32] Clearly Lippmann had in mind the possibilities of such a system for the purchase of elections.

It is doubtful if anyone could surpass Hiram Johnson's credentials as a progressive in the 1930s. His name was virtually synonymous with the progressive movement in early 1900s California, and he was equally progressive on the Washington scene as a Republican Senator from that state. In 1912 he abandoned the Republican Party to run as vice presidential candidate on the Progressive Party ticket with Theodore Roosevelt. His failure to campaign in California for the 1916 GOP presidential candidate, Charles Evans Hughes, was generally blamed for Hughes's defeat in that state and for Woodrow Wilson's reelection.

In state and national politics, Johnson harbored an anathema towards his fellow Californian, Herbert Hoover. He unsuccessfully opposed Hoover's appointment to Harding's cabinet and remained alienated from him through Hoover's commerce years and the presidency. In 1932 he abandoned the Republican ticket to campaign for FDR as a "Progressive for Roosevelt" along with fellow progressives like Harold Ickes, Amos Pinchot, and George Norris.

Roosevelt demonstrated his appreciation for Johnson's support early in his presidency by the frequent social contacts he arranged between their two families, and his solicitation of the Californian's advice on issues. These early contacts impressed Johnson with the president's energy, optimism, and open-mindedness. Soon after the inauguration, Johnson wrote to his sons that he could "not see how any living soul can last physically going the pace that [Roosevelt] is going, and mentally any one of us would be a psychopathic case if we undertook to do what he is doing." Yet despite it all, Roosevelt never showed "anything but the utmost good nature."[33]

A few days later, he wrote again that the White House was now occupied by "a regular human being." He cautioned, however, that this might not continue, since "the position with all its powers and its innumerable courtiers, not only destroys one's sense of human values, but has the most evil effects upon the shrinking, or timid, or small individual."[34] In the meantime, however, he found Roosevelt's policies "nearer to our philosophy of government than we have ever seen in my lifetime in this nation."[35] Similarly, a fellow progressive Republican senator, James Couzens of Michigan, was writing that he had "served in Washington under four presidents and . . . Roosevelt is the only one who has indicated a keen interest in the common people whom Lincoln pleaded for."[36]

A Johnson biographer, Richard Coke Lower, writes that Johnson accepted the fact that billions might have to be spent, perhaps even wasted, in order to provide relief, despite the unprecedented power given to Roosevelt.[37] Johnson did not, however, vote for all of the New Deal legislation of the hundred days. He voted against the National Industrial Recovery Act, for the bill did not include safeguards against monopolistic practices that he and some other liberals favored. And although he voted for the Agricultural Adjustment Act, with the inflationary Thomas Amendment, he opposed other inflationary bills including Roosevelt's Gold Bill.[38]

Three months into the New Deal, however, Johnson found Roosevelt "losing a little of his astounding and remarkable poise, and I rather think a bit of his extreme good nature. There is a revolt in the air in the Congress, too."[39] And he began to express mild reservations, writing that there was "hostility and bitterness" being revealed toward the New Deal even by Democrats.[40] A year into the New Deal, Johnson was commenting on Roosevelt's "extraordinary cunning," and he found himself opposing the president over the Reciprocal Tariff Bill, since he regarded it as a "gross surrender" of congressional authority to the White House that the Democrats had refused to grant Hoover in 1929.[41] Six months later, Johnson expressed himself as "extremely troubled about [Roosevelt's] demand for Four Billion Dollars un-earmarked," but willing to vote him the money because had no plan of his own to deal with the "country's ills." He was worried, however, about the "possible effect upon our sort of parliamentary government" of entrusting the executive with such a large discretionary fund.[42] And six weeks later he wrote that, while he retained his "high regard for the President," he was "worried about his course, and more troubled about his knowledge of his course."[43]

Johnson's relations with FDR first began to sour during the congressional elections of 1934, when the administration supported Democrat Dennis Chavez in the New Mexico senatorial race against progressive Republican Bronson Cutting who, like Johnson, had deserted his party's presidential nominee to campaign for Roosevelt in 1932. Roosevelt's desertion of Cutting rankled Johnson, and when the electoral results were disputed and thrown into the lap of the Senate for decision, Johnson obtained a seat on the Senate Elections Committee. He also interceded with Roosevelt, but found the president deaf to his pleas. During a flight to Washington with affidavits supporting his cause—a flight that would not have been necessary had it not been for the tangle the administration had woven—Cutting was killed in a plane crash. When Chavez subsequently took Cutting's seat in the Senate, Johnson and other progressive Republicans left the chamber in protest.[44]

A second issue between Johnson and the president was the World Court. Johnson and William Borah had been opponents of American involvement in any such international bodies since their battles against the League of Nations Covenant in 1919–1920, and their opposition had not lessened when the court came before the Senate early in 1935. Roosevelt, apparently certain that the bill would pass, promised Johnson that the White House would take no active role in support of the bill. Initially, it seemed that the opponents were doomed to defeat. Then the opposition outside the Senate mounted and votes within were swayed. Belatedly, Roosevelt violated his pledge to Johnson and supported the bill, but to no avail. The bill failed to gather the two-third vote necessary for American adherence, but Johnson felt betrayed.[45]

It was Roosevelt's "must" tax bill of 1935, however, which began for the first time to raise serious doubts in Johnson about the president he had helped to elect. He wrote an agonized letter to his son on 29 June that Roosevelt had "really kicked his foot in the mode with which he went at his tax bill." The philosophy behind the bill was not the chief cause of opposition, but rather his endeavor to bludgeon it through in two or three days without either preparation, or study, or knowledge of detail." Even the newspapers normally friendly to the administration had joined for the first time in the berating and Roosevelt had increased the feeling of uncertainty about him, especially where " his sense of proportion and his ideas of policies" were concerned. Johnson lamented the absence of a viable Republican Party and the lack of candidate who could oppose the president. As for the raids on the federal treasury by various interests under the New Deal, Johnson worried that it was creating "a terrible psychology" among the people that would continue to "plague the country long after he was dead."[46]

A month later, he renewed his criticism, complaining of the "many petty annoyances from those about Roosevelt," the lack of realism among his advisers, and the obvious scheme to use relief money to buy votes. But in weighing the advantages against the disadvantages of the Roosevelt administration, Johnson still thought "we can balance the ledger greatly to his credit."[47] And Johnson supported most of the New Deal legislative initiatives of 1935, including the Public Utility Holding Company Act, the Wagner Labor Act, and the Social Security Act.

A fellow progressive Republican Senator, Charles McNary of Oregon, had, however, begun to harbor reservations about the likelihood of recovery under the New Deal, writing that he found a widespread feeling of "unrest and uncertainty" as to the administration's policies that could be cured if only Roosevelt "would make a statement concerning his program so that business could adjust itself thereto." He found Roosevelt still popular in the western states, but "growing criticism of the administration."[48] A colleague agreed that he could not detect a coherent program in the New Deal hodgepodge. He wrote, "There is a new phrase which apparently has been coined called 'social capitalism' and perhaps that, properly defined, will be what we will get." Still, he was reluctant to criticize Roosevelt, because he had vivid memories of the impotence that had existed before he became president.[49]

— 3 —

The Combatants

Louis Brandeis continued to loom large as an influence on liberalism into the 1930s from his position on the Supreme Court and through the assorted Brandeisians placed in the Roosevelt administration by Harvard law professor Felix Frankfurter. As Brandeis described his program to a visitor,

First, I would take the Government out of the hands of the bankers. I would do that by opening the [federal] postal savings departments to all depositors without limitations of amount. I would establish in the post offices also a checking department, so that the post office could be used for commercial accounts. I should also make the postal department the agency for the issuance of securities. By appropriate federal taxation, I would split up the banking business into its separate parts and prohibit any bank from doing any more than one kind of banking business. . . . This would avoid the evil of great concentration of financial power in the hands of bankers. Secondly, by appropriate federal taxation I would limit the amount of property which any person could acquire or pass down upon death. . . . Thirdly, by appropriate federal excise taxes I would limit the size of corporations. I would do it not only with respect to corporations to be formed in the future, but also for existing corporations.[1]

This was a set of proposals almost as radical as those of the collectivist liberals. It contemplated federal competition with the banking industry in virtually every aspect of that business, federal control of the securities business, and the use of the taxing power of the federal government as a club with which to beat banking down even further, and along with it individual wealth and corporate size. Unlike the collectivists, however, Brandeis did not contemplate the destruction of the free enterprise system, and was opposed to central planning, but even the collectivists within the administration could welcome the powers that would be given to the federal government over business and banking under such a fantastic scheme. To place control of the flotation of stocks and bonds in the post office department, for example, the most political of all agencies of the federal government, opened a myriad of opportunities for the dictation of conditions under which businesses might have access to funds raised through such equities. Private business, operating under such conditions, would be scarcely freer than that operating under fascism in Italy.

In most ways, however, the views of Louis Brandeis seemed anachronistically representative of a traditional liberalism that had few spokesmen in the 1930s. Even Felix Frankfurter, regarded as Brandeis's disciple and the principal spokesman of his views, had abandoned many of them for those of the collectivist liberals, largely under the influence of the British Marxist, Harold Laski, and was actively pressing these antithetical views on the Roosevelt administration.[2] The Brandeisian position desperately needed an articulate spokesman more committed to it than Frankfurter if it were to compete with the collectivist liberals for the ear of the president. That spokesman, it soon developed, was to be David Cushman Coyle.

Coyle had been educated as an engineer at Rensselear Polytechnic Institute and had worked thereafter as a consulting engineer. During the 1920s a great many engineers were converted to a belief that economic problems were susceptible to engineering solutions, a view that led to the short-lived technocrat movement in the late 1920s and early 1930s. Coyle, too, managed to convince himself that he was an economist with the solution to the nation's economic ills. He published several articles and pamphlets that contained his analysis of the causes of the depression and his prescription for not only generating recovery, but also for preventing any further such downturns in the business cycle. Those articles and pamphlets, and the unorthodox ideas they contained, would probably have attracted little attention had it not been for the support he received initially from Felix Frankfurter. Indeed, Frankfurter's effort to promote Coyle's ideas even predated Roosevelt's inauguration, when the Harvard law professor exerted himself to obtain publicity for Coyle's writings and to ensure that they received favorable reviews in the media. These two amateur economists—the one a consulting engineer whose letterhead listed the specialities of "Buildings," "Foundations," and "Wind Vibration Tests," and the other a law professor—shared in common a lack of appreciation for economic orthodoxy and a willingness to undertake liberal experiments in economic affairs.

Coyle first attracted Frankfurter's attention with an article entitled, "Business and Finance" that he published in *Corporate Practice Review* in mid-1932. After reading the article, Frankfurter wrote its author that he had "the feeling that one has when clear air and sunshine break into a dank room." Coyle had "shown more shrewdly and comprehensively than I have seen in any single piece of writing how anachronistic are the economic assumptions which underlie the essential efforts of Washington and Wall Street to deal with the depression from any long-range point of view."[3] Encouraged, Coyle sought Frankfurter's help in publishing and distributing "an enlarged form" of the article as a pamphlet. Frankfurter then busied himself with promoting Coyle's views and distributing reprints of the article.[4]

The pamphlet was entitled, *The Irrepressible Conflict: Business and Finance*. In the preface, Coyle explained that his article had "received so many favorable comments that it has been considered desirable to reprint the material, with revisions to meet changed conditions, and with explanations and illustrations of points that were not clear in its more condensed form." His intention, Coyle wrote, was not to present "a detailed plan for a new social order," but to promote "a new orientation of thought." In the early years of the Republic, he observed, "frugality and hard work held the only hope of surival." Money at that time had to be diverted from spending by consumers and into the hands of financiers who could "use it to build factories, and later to develop railroads and great cities." Quite naturally, Americans had continued to cling to those traditional virtues, and were now dismayed that they seemed powerless against the depression. The problem, Coyle observed, was that America was a different place from 1790, and the "insistent demand" now was "not for labor, not for capital, but for buyers to carry away the goods." Recovery and a healthy economy depended on renewed spending for consumer goods. "The central economic law of the power age," Coyle wrote, "is that business cannot stand too much capital. . . . It is evident that the moral precepts of Benjamin Franklin do not fit the necessities of times like these. From now on, the intolerable sin is not extravagance, but avarice." What was needed was the power to direct money "away from any form of investment whatever." Planning was obviously necessary, but "simply planning the first thing that comes to hand is not the answer."[5]

In his pamphlet, Coyle examined and rejected the various proposals for planning the United States out of the depression. One popular proposal, with some businessmen and politicians, involved various degrees of cartelization, with or without governmental involvement. Written before Roosevelt's election and inauguration, Coyle's views on cartelization are interesting in light of the National Industrial Recovery Act which was pushed through Congress during the hundred days. Of cartelization, Coyle wrote that "controlling the volume of production and preventing a fall of price" was "a positive plan that goes directly at the instability of prices which is so injurious to any business." However, the negative effects were injurious to the "uncartelized" segment of the economy, shifting deflation to "consumers' incomes, i.e., in the only source of business, with the result that the last state of industry is worse than the first." Such a system could operate effectively only if it could "fix prices, wages, and incomes to keep consumption up to production, which makes it technically indistinguishable from the communist state," and it was "questionable whether the American people are temperamentally suited to militarized planning, and whether we could easily find rulers with enough vitality to stand up to us."[6]

Coyle then proposed his own solution. The problem was over-saving—too much money going into investments, many of them worthless, rather than into consumer purchases, or, as Coyle put it, to Wall Street rather than to Main Street. The solution was to divert money from investment and into consumer purchasing power. As Coyle put it: "The traditional method of directing the flow of money from one part of the economic system to another is by use of the tax system. Taxes are the most powerful pump we know of." The cost of high taxes on the wealthy was not passed onto the consumer, but to "the promoter and the bond house," since they left less money available for investment. Above a specified ceiling on income "practically all the surplus income" would be taken except that which had been contributed to charitable purposes.[7]

Coyle then explained why business and finance were in an "irrepressible conflict."

The normal processes of finance are poisonous to business. . . . Business needs stability to prosper; finance gets its profits from instability. To be more specific: the income tax makes for stability and hurts finance; the sales tax makes for instability and hurts business. Over this conflict of interest there must be a battle, because so long as finance dominates business both are headed for the precipice, and finance will not loose its grip without a fight. . . . The crossroads of history will be the place where we do or do not develop means for keeping money out of Wall Street and making it travel up and down Main Street where it belongs.[8]

Coyle dismissed any consideration of a collectivist solution to the nation's problems, writing, "Among our people dynamic emotion attaches to the idea of freedom of initiative. . . . [T]he communist solution, while mathematically sound, is fatally handicapped, for us, by our temperamental distaste for discipline." Sounding very Brandeisian, Coyle argued that it was vital to promote the interests of "middle-sized concerns" in order to provide "openings for individual initiative and leadership."[9] All other issues, however, were subordinate to the essential one of "the distribution of income and the allocation of income between equipment and consumption. . . . The master plan of the economic system for a power age will necessarily be a plan for directing the flow of money. All other plans are either supplementary to their central objective or else inconsequential." Money must be diverted "from investment in commercial equipment to the consumption of the goods that business is trying to sell."[10] Coyle's views would be more influential beginning in 1935.

Harold Laski's acquaintance with Roosevelt apparently dated from his years as a young history professor at Harvard, 1916–1920. While there, Laski embroiled himself in what should have been a relatively minor controversy by championing the cause of the Boston police in their famous strike that catapulted Calvin Coolidge into national attention. According to one source, there was a possibility that Laski might be dismissed from the Harvard faculty, but that Roosevelt, who was then a member of the Board of Overseers of the university, prevented it by threatening to resign if Laski were forced out. A friendship between the two naturally ensued, and Laski also made other fruitful friendships while at Harvard, including those with Justice Holmes and Harvard law professor Felix Frankfurter.[11] Nevertheless, Laski felt uncomfortable at Harvard and left for the London School of Economics, part of the University of London, in 1920. A torrent of essays and books began to issue from his pen. The transition through which his political philosophy went during these years need not concern us. From early on, however, Laski revealed an anticapitalist bias that grew more extreme as the years passed, and eventually progressed to a thoroughgoing Marxism. According to Arthur Schlesinger, the British general strike of 1926 "strengthened a growing belief that in moments of stress, capitalism would always turn against democracy."[12] Yet in that same year, Louis Brandeis wrote his daughter, after a visit by Laski, that he was "one of the few surviving who hold Felix's and my views on current American problems."[13] It was perhaps an outcome of Laski's ability, as Edmund Wilson put it, to draw "a curtain or screen in front of his Marxism" and spend "the evening on the liberal basis."[14]

Typical of his views were those contained in an essay, "Can Business Be Civilized," that appeared in a volume of his essays in 1930. Said Laski, "in the period since the Industrial Revolution brought the business man to his unexampled supremacy, the one great lesson we have grimly learned is the utter inadequacy of the profit-making motive to build a well-ordered society," nor had it shown itself consistent "with the achievement of an adequate life." Laski continued,

It is obvious that the mere acquisition of property is not a noble end; and a society, therefore, in which the profit-making motive determines the general temper has lost the clue whereby civilization may be found. . . . The condition is a determination on our part to make the principles of industrial organization definitely referable to a moral end. Those who labor in business, that is to say, must regard themselves not as merely concerned with personal gain, but as servants of a function the purpose of which is the release of society from the conflict with nature. But to serve a function is to be no longer a master. To serve a function is to admit that the property one receives, the orders one issues, are all of them explicable in terms of reason . . . it is obvious that the present distribution of wealth both to functionless owners and to men whose immense gains are unrelated to true service is an outstanding and indefensible scandal.

Without ownership, management and labor were alike in that each was a participant in the function of the industry, "but once the element of ownership is introduced, the allegiance of the manager is deflected away from the social context of production—the basis of rationality in business—over to the service he is compelled to offer to the profit-making motive." Laski concluded:

As we stand now, our feet are near the abyss. We cannot avoid the danger of conflict so long as we fail to abolish the tyranny of man over man. We cannot abolish that tyranny where our idea of property confers rights without duties, claims without obligation to serve. The condition of our well-being is fellowship; and this is possible only where men are won to a common service.[15]

There were echoes of Laski's views in Roosevelt's 1933 inaugural address and in other speeches.

In April 1931, Laski delivered a series of lectures at the University of North Carolina, and, as became a common practice, he published these lectures, with revisions, as a book, *Democracy in Crisis*, in 1933. In that book, Laski defined the principle of democracy as "the assertion that men and women have an equal claim upon the common good; that, therefore, no social order can for long endure in which that principle is inherenty denied." He continued:

The question . . . we have to answer is not whether democracy will survive, but whether capitalist democracy will survive, for that is the system which is attacked. For the masses, I believe, it is not attacked because it is regarded as inherently wrong, though that is the main motive of its outstanding critics; it is attacked because it is unsuccessful. The results it can now secure do not justify the claims made upon its behalf. And a social order that is in decay is like a beleaguered city, every place in its defences appears a contingent point of attack.

The assumption that a change in the basic character of a social order seems unlikely of accomplishment without violence is a challenge to two convictions which lie at the very heart of the liberal temper. It seems to deny the primacy of reason as a method of resolving social differences, and it visualises an atmosphere in which liberty as the expression of a constitutional system is deliberately put aside in the period of consolidation.

Capitalism today is in the position of a church which hears blasphemy within its walls, and it moves to persecution through its appointed organs exactly as in an earlier age and upon a different field.

Laski then renewed his attack on the profit motive: "Certainly no one can now seriously maintain that the profit-making motive is the fundamental root of social good....The discipline of capitalist democracy is in decay because the principle of capitalism cannot be squared with the principle of democracy."

Capitalism could prevail in an expanding economy, Laski suggested, because it could improve the standard of living of the masses, but in a contracting economy, such as was the case during the depression, this was not an option. In a contracting economy there were attacks "upon vested interests which make these angry and fearful before the adjustments demanded," and

There is too little time for the psychological conditions of acceptance by consent to be prepared. Only under such conditions are men capable of arriving at their accomodations in terms of reason; in other conditions, because the price exacted for the new equilibrium is exacted so quickly, is so directly contrasted with the habits they have known, acceptance by consent becomes, at best, a matter of grave dubiety. . . . Acquiescence in abdication is in any case rare where the stake in dispute is the rights of property. . . . And a succession of serious outbreaks, suppressed only at heavy cost, would so endanger the economic success of the new system that an original communist victory might be followed by a decade of conflict in which . . . the impoverishment of the community might well render impossible over a long period . . . a new equilibium in which men accept those established expectations which make for social peace. . . . The only way to postpone the issue is by discovering anew the terms of economic prosperity and so increasing the material benefits in which the masses can participate.[16]

If this were so, nothing could be more futile than efforts at reform. For Laski it could delay, but must inevitably result in, the transition to collectivism it was designed to prevent.[17]

Shortly before the 1932 election, Laski wrote Frankfurter that he had just completed "a little book" that was "a philosophic–historic explanation of why capitalism and democracy are incompatible; with a discussion of how the institutions of capitalist democracy being built on inescapable contradictions issue inevitably into revolution." Laski thought it "the most creative book I have ever written," and he hoped more for Frankfurter's "agreement with it than I know easily how to say. I even believe it may cause Walter [Lippmann] moments of acute discomfort, though perhaps this is too big a claim." He was watching the American election "with fevered anxiety." He did not consider Roosevelt's a "great campaign; but at least he has recognised the existence of the common man. I want him to get in with a narrow majority, [Norman] Thomas getting some two to three million votes." A few weeks later he wondered "which Roosevelt is going to enter the White House."[18]

In January 1933, Laski greeted the approaching inauguration of Franklin Delano Roosevelt with a fair amount of skepticism, but a conviction that opportunities existed if the new president would but grasp them. He wrote in *Living Age,*

I agree with those who think that, temperamentally, there is a real liberal somewhere in Mr. Roosevelt. But, looking at the Democratic Party, I suspect that it will have to make a rapid and decisive appearance if it is going to be effective in his term. If it did make its appearance, there are forces to spare in America of which Mr. Roosevelt could make ample use. The United States of the slump is skeptical, inclined to experiment, uneasy about the confident faith in laissez-faire that did duty for thought in times of prosperity.

The business man's philosophy no longer has the primacy of old; it has been tried and found sadly wanting. All the best minds of America, [John] Dewey and Morris Cohen in philosophy, Brandeis, Stone, and Frankfurter in law, Taussig and Hamilton in economics, Edmund Wilson, Dreiser,

Lewis, and Dos Passos in letters, are on the radical side. If Mr. Roosevelt has the will to choose their direction, the courage to walk in their path, with his satisfactory majority in Congress, with the prospect of making a liberal majority on the Supreme Court, he might make his presidency an epoch in American history.

Someone has got to convince him that the day of the old platitudes is gone. . . . There has got to be born a sense of the state, an understanding that liberty begins only where equality begins, a conviction that the nation, and not a little group of millionaires, has henceforth to be the master of the nation's destinies.

While admitting that the light vote for the Socialist candidate, Norman Thomas, showed that there was "as yet no workers' party in America, and only the beginnings of a working-party consciousness," Laski nevertheless wrote:

No doubt, there is a profound idealism in America, a latent radicalism also which, in the newfound temper of skepticism, a great statesman could canalize into a deepening stream of support. But to do so he would have to fight the industrial autocracy of the South, the power of Wall Street, a Democratic Party, large parts of which still dwell in the Middle Ages, the corrupt interests of state and municipal government, the vested interests of the gangsters. It is a big fight to take on.

Well, there is fighting blood in the Roosevelts, and it may be that early antagonism will arouse it in the new President. If he chooses the harder way, he has an opportunity as great as any president since Lincoln; I add that posterity salutes the man who chooses the harder way. If he chooses it, he can find the counselors to give him the ideas, to show the direction, to stand by him with wisdom and courage.[19]

Clearly, Laski was willing to enlist.

In August Laski wrote Frankfurter that he had penned an article on Brandeis for *Harper's* magazine. He added,

We follow your "revolution" with absorbed interest. From here it looks like touch and go. I can't pretend to more than the sympathy of half understanding. It looks to me as though F. R. still underestimates the opposition which will organize against him at the first opportunity. But without the feel of your opinion I can only guess in a darkness. At least he has energy and courage. . . . I was amused at Amos [Pinchot's] attacks on W. L. [Lippmann]. They had a point; but they were really too crude to be effective. I saw [Lippmann] in London just before I left for Spain. What impressed me was his anxiety to be used by the administration. He continually insisted that F. R. ought to use the men who know, regardless of whether they had been against his nomination; and he was distressed that you did not share this view.[20]

In February 1934, with the New Deal less than a year old, Laski submitted "The Roosevelt Experiment" to analysis in the pages of *Atlantic*, writing that the president was

the first statesman in a great capitalist society who has sought deliberately and systematically to use the power of the state to subordinate the primary assumptions of that society to certain vital social purposes. He is the first statesman deliberately to experiment on a wholesale scale with the limitation of the profit-making motive. He is the first statesman, again in a wholesale way, to attack not the secondary but the primary manifestations of the doctrine of laissez faire. He is the first statesman who, of his own volition, and without coercion, either direct or indirect, has placed in the hands of organized labor a weapon which, if it be used successfully, is bound to result in a vital readjustment of the relative bargaining power of Capital and Labor. He is also the first statesman who, the taxing power apart, has sought to use the political authority of the state to compel, over the whole area of economic effort, a significant readjustment of the national income.

Roosevelt had displayed "a creative audacity, a sense of psychological essentials, an eye for the pivotal matters involved, which deserve well of the commonwealth he seeks to serve. Russia . . . apart, there has been no adventure of comparable range or intensity in modern times." Laski wondered, however, "what the implications of his adventure actually are, and the relation of these to the total social situation in which he finds himself involved. For it is dangerous to experiment with the foundations of a society unless the experiment be built upon doctrinal assumptions the conclusions of which follow with irresistible logic from the premises it is legitimate to use."

Yet Roosevelt's policies seemed to him based less on radicalism than "sober conservatism." It was obvious to Laski that the president was "feeling his way to a policy which has assumed no final shape in his mind; and it is equally obvious that until he knows what he does want there is no prospect of any serious revival in trade." Those policies represented

a profound wave of half-articulate protest against the character of contemporary American capitalism. . . . The Roosevelt experiment, in a word, is a systematic effort to put capitalism into leading strings of principle. It is to be the servant, and not the master, of the American people. . . . It is inevitable, sooner or later, in any society built upon universal suffrage that the people should use its political power to mitigate the consequences of unrestricted capitalism; and severe disaster, like that which has characterized the last four years, only stimulates that temper more intensely. . . . The remarkable thing about his innovations is not their size, but the immediacy of their relations to the traditional liberalism of America . . . even if they wholly succeed, no radical would be tempted to regard them as anything more than a necessary historic phase in the slow evolution [*sic*] of American capitalism. . . . But the object of the reforms is no less than to destroy the unlimited power of American capitalism to shape the contours of American life. It is to end the unbridled individualism of Mr. Ford; it is to break in pieces the industrial feudalism of the baron of coal and steel. . . . Historically, it has never been the habit of a class voluntarily to abdicate from power. That has always been accomplished, as in 1789 in France, or in 1917 in Russia, by violence, or, as in England in 1832, by the threat of violence the success of which was overwhelmingly probable.[21]

A month later, Laski reviewed the dangers to freedom in the world and wrote in the *Yale Review*:

Where a society . . . is insecure it must reform itself; for only in this way can it deal with the causes of its insecurity. No doubt, this implies great sacrifices from those who, whether from effort or good fortune, have dwelt at ease in Zion. But the alternative to sacrifice is conflict; and of this no man can predict either the outcome or the end. In a civilization like ours, where the common man has tasted political power, it is psychologically inevitable that he should use his authority to increase his share in the common stock. He may be persuaded to postpone his demand because the success of the regime offers him a continually increasing prospect of good. But once that prospect diminishes, he will refuse to believe that the mere conflict of private interests will produce a well-ordered commonwealth. That is why the growth of democracy has meant increasing social regulation. That is why, also, when the margins of concession under capitalist democracy are reached, the movement to socialism gathers a momentum so profound. We can meet the movement by reasoned discussion, which means a gradual but definite adjustment of policy to demand. Or we can meet it with resistance. In the latter event, in more or less degree we create a Fascist dictatorship; and where that proves unable to satisfy the economic demands it encounters, the logical outcome is communist dictatorship. For in the conflict of extremes men are too passionate to give heed to the call of the Mean.[22]

Laski repeated the thesis in an essay for *The American Scholar*: "Not even the years before the War of 1914 have imposed so tense a strain upon men's minds as the period since the advent of Hitler to power. The conventions upon which our civilization has been built are challenged at their foundation."

The outstanding feature of our time is insecurity. Epochs of this character—witness the Reformation and the French Revolution—have always been unfavorable to reason and tolerance; they have therefore been epochs in which dictatorship has its opportunity. And men always feel insecure when their privileges are challenged. They are not prepared to accept the invasion of their wonted routines. They seek to make their private claims universal rights; and those who provide them with the means of enforcing their claims are regarded as their saviors.

This was the case now, in the 1930s, when the economic contraction of the Great Depression, combined with political democracy, was threatening the privileges of the "haves," who believed in democracy only so long as it could be manipulated by them. Faced with a choice between preserving their privileges and property and preserving democracy, the "haves" invariably jettisoned democracy, as had happened in Germany and Italy. As Laski put it, "It seems that the forms of private property . . . must not be touched by the normal operations of political democracy." If they were threatened, then "business men will cooperate in the destruction of democracy as ardently as they cooperated in the destruction of feudalism in the centuries between the Reformation and the French Revolution. . . . The middle class is just as accustomed to rule as its predecessor, the feudal aristocracy. It would regard its displacement from privilege as a no less momentous disaster to society ."[23]

In February 1935, Laski wrote Frankfurter that he would be in the United States from late March until late April, and "except for Mondays (New School) and April 10–11 (Illinois) I shall be at your disposal. I want a week-end in Yale (round April 18) and some days in Washington (can I have an hour with F.D.R.) otherwise I propose to stay with you both as long as you will have me." He added, "Be careful with the N.R. [New Republic] people. I think they 'growl' too much without putting a feasible alternative. But no one must do anything just now to discourage a critical spirit. Freedom is too tenuous in its hold to [be] spanked even when it is less helpful than it might be."[24]

Also, in February 1935, Laski published an essay on "Discretionary Power" in *Politica*, and defined discretionary power as "the conferment upon the executive of an authority . . . which it is free to exercise as it thinks fit." The practice, he pointed out, had burgeoned in both America and England since World War I, and there were doubts about its wisdom "not only because of its evident encouragement to bureaucracy, but also because, by developing the executive, at the expense of the legislative power, it becomes closely allied to those changes in the systems of government which, as most notably in Central and South-Eastern Europe, have ended in dictatorship." In this respect, Laski had clearly in mind the abuses of Article 48 of the Weimar Constitution which had paved the way to dictatorship in Germany. But increased discretionary power was a necessary result, he wrote, of the transformation from the negative state, whose "very range of . . . purposes no longer permitted the legislature to give any serious attention to problems of detail," to the positive one. So complicated had matters become, in fact, that without the increase in discretionary powers "modern governments would be procedurally bankrupt." What was important was to safeguard the practice against abuses. Unfortunately, in the sphere of social legislation, governments typically encountered "the too fixed rights of private property which are protected by the courts with quite insufficient regard to the social consequences they involve." This, in Laski's view, rendered "the ordinary courts unsuitable to control the exercise of discretionary powers" because they lacked "the elasticity and the social insight now essential if these powers are to attain their appointed end." It required special courts and special men capable of dealing with such cases.[25] There must also be procedures built in for the fullest scrutiny of the acts of those granted such discretionary powers, that they might not be abused.

Soon thereafter Laski visited the United States and debated former brain truster Adolf Berle at the New School for Social Research in New York on the topic "Has Democracy Vitality Today." Laski insisted that the marriage between democracy and capitalism had reached the point where either capitalism must suppress democracy or democracy must transform capitalism. When political democracy began to act in the economic field "the governing classes began to realize that the only durable source of power is property," and that if it were faced with a choice it would choose its possessions. In this choice lay the beginnings of fascism, for it marked "the deliberate choice by men of the overthrow of government, lest democracy overthrow their possessions."[26] A month later he visited Roosevelt, telling reporters that he and the president had known each other since he taught at Harvard.[27] After his return to England, Laski delivered his observations on the American scene in an article for the London *Daily Herald*, in which he wrote the following:

The tragedy of America is the absence of any common American ideology of the Left at a time when its presence is the one real safeguard against the victory of conservatism by default. The result is that there is no organized power behind any of the things the radicals know to be essential. They destroy the things they might enforce by their inability to sink their differences in the front of the common foe. They sacrifice immediate urgencies to ultimate ideologies. The President understands the first; he is utterly remote from the second.

The Left has the chance of taking the offensive; but to do so it must make the impact of unity. To fail to achieve this means to be defeated just as it was defeated in the textile strike and in San Francisco.

It is no use blaming the President for not sharing the ideals of (Socialist) Norman Thomas or (Communist) W. Z. Foster. If he shared them, he would not be President of the United States. The thing to do is to affirm the radicals' platform with such emphasis that the President is driven by their impact to turn in their direction. He will not, in any case, turn the whole way. But, if the American radicals knew their job, he would turn far enough in their way to give them the chance of taking the initiative in the next years. As it is, they deprive themselves of the main influence they could exert by making their mutual hostilities far more apparent than their common agreement—that the social system in America to-day is bankrupt.

For the first time since 1787 the validity of the American Constitution is directly in question. As it has been put by the Supreme Court, the problem is whether the State has the power at its disposal to govern in terms of modern needs. If the radicals know their job, they can put that problem upon a basis that will completely alter the perspective of American politics.

If they fail (and the present disunity makes failure a grave possibility), the victory of Wall Street is certain. If they succeed in overcoming their differences, they may make the latent sentiment for fundamental change articulate for the first time in America. That would open a new epoch in the history of the world.[28]

Changes were taking place both within liberalism and within the Roosevelt administration. In 1935, *TNR* examined the new liberalism in an essay, "Liberalism Twenty Years After." "The essence of political and economic liberty in the twentieth-century industrial state," it wrote, had evolved from the laissez faire preached by Adam Smith and John Stuart Mill "to a powerful interventionism. In delegating political power to elected officials, Americans needed to exert utmost care, particularly since the onset of centralized planning would concentrate power in the hands of a small group of planners and open the door to the possibility of "virtual dictatorship."

Coining a new word—transvalued liberalism—for its new views, *TNR* embraced all those—even including socialists and communists—who were committed to creating "a collective society."[29] In an ad to attract subscribers, *TNR* noted late in 1935 that it was "not affiliated with any political party. It has criticized many aspects of the New Deal and has praised some others. For its own political program it favors an approach toward collectivism through a genuine labor party."[30]

The publication of Laski's book, *The State in Theory and Practice*, inspired a number of reviews, which, while admiring of its author and the breadth of his work, found deficiencies in a book that was so obviously crafted to advance the argument for socialism. Laski indicted the modern state as a representation of the interests of the moneyed classes under the liberalism that was especially a product of the Industrial Revolution, criticizing it both for its domestic and international shortcomings. While most liberals regarded it as an act of faith that democracy could not exist in any other but a free economy, Laski insisted that, on the contrary, democracy and capitalism were incompatible. Yet, he seemed pessimistic that the socialist society he advocated showed any sign of early fruition, despite the promising conditions offered by the upheaval of the depression. He wrote, "In our own time the conditions of fundamental changes are present; but we seem likely to fail to utilize them, less because there is disagreement upon objectives than because there is disunity about the methods whereby the objectives can be maintained."[31]

An unflattering review by William Yandell Elliott in the *Southern Review* linked Laski to Frankfurter, and via Frankfurter to the White House. Elliott wrote that Laski's "persuasiveness, dialectic power, and . . . stylist brilliance have given his views the widest currency in academic circles. . . . Literally thousands of American students have enjoyed his genial gossip, full of the most intimate anecdotes of his influence on great men and weighty affairs. Through Felix Frankfurter, his influence on the Roosevelt administration has been far from negligible."

Describing Laski, however, as "a political pamphleteer rather than a philosopher," Elliott accused him of playing "fast and loose with all sorts of inconsistent values" that contradicted the premise of his reasoning.

With enormous ingenuity and the persuasiveness which make him such an outstanding political partisan, Mr. Laski has striven to hitch this Marxian apparatus on to the liberal philosophy of individual rights and constitutional protections. The effort has involved him in feats of casuistry worthy of the great acrobatic traditions of the classical apologists. . . . Today one would not be far wrong in describing him as a communist of doctrine but not of declaration. He still feels that the time is not ripe for a show-down, and that the communists had better make common cause with social-democrats against fascism. But he does not, today, have a real hope that democratic methods, without direct action on a revolutionary scale, will produce the society that he holds to be ethically necessary, and ultimately destined to be realized.

But, Elliott added, Laski's Marxism was forcing him "reluctantly to renounce his libertarian doctrines," for

One cannot insist on suppressing a considerable part of a given society and on changing its institutions by, if necessary, violent means, and still cherish the protection of constitutionalism. And what becomes of the liberty to disagree—if one disagrees entirely with Marx and Mr. Laski on the nature of political justice in the economic realm? Many people still do not accept this gospel—apparently a majority do not. Is that why Mr. Laski despairs of democracy?

The reason for spending so much time on the case of Mr. Laski lies in the fact that he is a prime example of a kind of so-called liberal thinking that is a very dangerous enemy to constitutional liberty for the very reason that it poses always as a friend. He represents a type of intellectual whose didactive brilliance as a pamphleteer has had a remarkable effect in an age of skillful publicists but an age of little profound critical thinking.[32]

An upset Laski wrote to Frankfurter: "Did you, by the way, see an essay in jealousy by W. Y. Elliott on me in the *Southern Quarterly* in which my private heresies were foully used to stage an attack on you. That nasty piece might be politely told that things are not done that way."[33]

Meanwhile, Max Ascoli had reviewed Laski's *The State in Theory and Practice* for *TNR*, heading his review "Retreat from Liberalism." Ascoli found Hitler Germany "haunting Harold Laski," with the result that for people like Laski "the fundamental task of political philosophy in our generation" was "the invention of barriers in the way of fascism." Ascoli continued,

Laski offers his answer: Hitler represents the last, unavoidable reaction of a decadent capitalism in an era when capitalism cannot stop its own decadence. Through Hitler's experiment the modern state has been conclusively proved a tool of class domination used by those who own the instruments of production. The only possible defense against fascism is radically changing the present economic order and installing the socialistic state.

These are very clear propositions, already inserted in the dogma of left-wing socialism all over the world. But when such schemes are reinvented and developed by a political scientist of Laski's vigor, their unfoldment brings to light all the underlying vital problems. This unscrupulous, decaying capitalism, which is destroying civilization in order to save itself, is, according to Laski, the focal point of all the evils of the modern state. So the fight that he formerly waged against sovereignty for the greater freedom of groups and individuals is now centered upon what he sees as the heart of the enemy. . . . It must be hard for a pluralist to double the power of the state by adding economic ownership to political sovereignty. But the struggle between democracy and capitalism, Laski asserts, is a fight to the finish. Even the sacrifice of political democracy, at least for a certain time, may be imperative.

Yet, in spite of the price he is willing to pay, Laski does not seem encouraged by many prospects of victory. Driven by what he considers the unavoidable pressure of events, he passes through positions that not long ago he defended, parts without bitterness from men who he understands, and reaches the front where the class war is waged according to criteria of Marxian intransigence. The whole way is trodden in a spirit of profound sincerity, almost of sadness. This retreat from liberalism has the character of an objective and unimpassioned autobiography. . . . His distrust of liberalism, possibly of reason, is implemented by the most reasonable man-to-man persuasion.

But Ascoli wondered if it were really true "that Hitler and Mussolini are the chieftains of a decadent capitalism, or are not they rather ruthless adventurers interjecting themselves into a deadlocked social struggle?" He wondered also if it was "really true that the ownership of the means of production determines the form and the action of the state, or is not rather true that the attempt to fight political battles in terms of class war leads to a deadlock and then to Hitler?" For all his problems with the book Ascoli considered it "the most compelling introduction to the debate of the post-Hitler political philosophy."[34]

— 4 —

Confusion in the Ranks

After the Supreme Court ruled against the NRA by a 9–0 vote that included Brandeis, Laski wrote Frankfurter that he was "appalled simply because it seems to me to open up the vistas opened up nearly eighty years ago by the Dred Scott case." He continued:

I know how it will be used by all the enemies of decency in our social constitution and I can't see any real way round. But the great thing for F.D.R. and people like you who are aware of its wide significance is to realize that it is an opportunity not less than a threat. Properly used, I think you can recover the support of organised labour by making it clear to them that the President will not give uncontrolled capitalism its head. From that angle I believe there is immense prestige in the use of the decision. I wish our friends on the Court had done something beyond mere concurrence. What hurts me most is the hardly concealed pleasure of the govt press here in the result. The govt. thinks it ends Roosevelt as a positive factor in social change. Conservatism courts disaster by blindness.[1]

A few days later Laski sent to Frankfurter copies of two letters he had mailed to Roosevelt advising him on how to respond to the decision.[2] The next day he wrote Roosevelt's secretary asking her to thank him for the "beautiful photograph" the president had given him. He added, "Meanwhile I hope you will tell him that the vital thing for him is to remember that famous telegram from Lord Acton to Mr. Gladstone when the Phoenix Park Murders seemed to wreck the possibility of pacification in Ireland 'Do not let him loose [sic] confidence in himself.'"[3] In November, FDR wrote that he hoped Laski would "come over here sometime this winter."[4] When Laski wrote that he would be visiting the United States for a month beginning the end of March 1936, FDR's secretary wrote that FDR "sends you his best wishes and wants you to be sure to come to see him when you get here early in April."[5] Laski did so.[6] Clearly, Laski was considered a desirable visitor at the White House.

Laski wrote Frankfurter that he was disturbed "by the news we get of your problems—not that I waver about F.D.R. as the main barrier against Fascism, but because there is no true coherence in his support—the old, terrible weakness of the Left. I imagine he is safe; but I now can't make out what he is safe for." He added, "I wish you would get a fellow of Tom Corcoran's quality to write a piece in Harper's on the actualities and potentialities. Reading the American press makes me feel that the position needs crystallisation into a body of principles, the kind of thing that the N[ew] R[epublic] and the Nation have to discuss from his angle and not theirs. Do think about this."[7]

In January Laski wrote FDR's secretary, "Will you tell him that I am sailing for America on the 11th March so that after the 18th I want to come and see him. There are so many things to talk about, not least his wisdom in deciding to make a direct attack on the Supreme Court. Incidentally in the light of his conference with the Newspaper Proprietors in March of 1936, I hope he has told Eugene Mayo [Meyer?] that the budget is in process of being balanced. I do not know whether this will cause Eugene more than surprise, perhaps, on balance the former."[8]

TNR was a consistent critic of the New Deal's welfare programs, including the W.P.A. The "political nepotism" that plagued the program, it observed, was the inevitable result of "the [James] Farley influence in the Roosevelt administration and will continue as long as the President accepts machine politics as a necessary condition to reelection." The W.P.A., it wrote, had been "a bad idea in the first place, and has been badly carried out," resulting in the waste of "huge sums and in creating an incalculable amount of human misery."[9] When the American Association of Social Workers declared at their annual conference that conditions in early 1936 were worse "than at any time during the Roosevelt administration or even . . . the last few months of Hoover's," *TNR* found it confirmation of its criticism of the WPA.[10]

TNR was also critical of the SEC for not making effective use of its authority. James Landis complained to Frankfurter that the charge was absurd, as the SEC had "used its power to a degree unparalleled by any administrative agency during any similar period of time."[11] Frankfurter responded with a long letter absolving himself of any connection with *TNR*'s editorial policies. He had resigned as a trustee after Croly's death, he told Landis, and, though he remained "on terms of warm friendship with both Bruce Bliven and George Soule—into whose hands fell the dominant direction of the paper," he did not feel "such a community of ideas and purpose with them that I should continue to have even formal responsibility for the paper." There were both "differences in outlook" and in "the means to be pursued for achieving common ends." He had not, he told Landis, read the issue that offended him, but he wanted "to do whatever I usefully can . . . to have them understand the good work that you and the Commission have been doing." Frankfurter assumed that "you are probably being pounded by people in the Street and especially their lawyers, for going too far and being too unreasonable, in at least equal measure as the quotations you give from the New Republic indicate that they are criticizing you for being too lenient and not going far enough." He wondered if perhaps the "thunder from the left doesn't serve as unconscious help against unreasonable demands from the right."[12] Some time later Landis dined with Bliven and Soule, thereby winning from them "a better understanding of what our work is, and what our objectives are, than they had before." He agreed with Frankfurter on the efficacy of "having an advance left wing, because if some of the pressure can be taken off by that type of an attack, naturally your advance will be more effective in the center," but he objected to the earlier *TNR* attack since it had "certain personal characteristics which weaken it from the standpoint of being able to help us."[13]

The confusion in which liberalism had fallen by 1936 as to its definition and objectives is well-illustrated by Justice Benjamin Cardozo's response to *The Rise of Liberalism*, when he wrote Laski, "I suppose there is no simple, all-sufficient definition of liberalism or any other social process. But the impressive lesson of this book is that every process is inadequate, however you define it, and that the best one can say of it is that it is an advance and an approach."[14]

A few weeks before the 1936 election, Laski wrote Frankfurter:

I need not say that we follow F.D.R.'s campaign with eager hope. I understand your restraint; but it does look to me that not even the money and the hatred are enough. I believe he will get a quite unexpectedly large majority, for Landon's speeches are so full of contradictions that I don't think he will touch more than the rentier and the small business men. Anyhow, three million is my prophecy. And I think I detect in the last week of F.D.R.'s speeches a sense that the thing is moving as you would wish. More, I think that Landon's confusions are the speeches of a beaten man. It was, by the way, really grand to have W[alter] L[ippmann] come out for the rich and laissez-faire. The more he is defined as a reactionary so that there can be no misunderstanding, the better I am pleased. These are days when men must be compelled to choose.[15]

After the election, Laski wrote that FDR's victory had been "beyond my wildest dreams. The people it disappointed were the measure of his achievement." He continued:

Now I want to see him show courage and energy and a sense of the central objective. I think the next four years may well be decisive in American history. For you either educate your masses to a sense of the right to hope, or you convince them that from the system as it is, there is no prospect of continuous improvement. It is in his hands as in no other man's; and he can be, like Lincoln, the architect of a great victory for righteousness or leave things in that despairing uncertainty that divides men into armies between which no reconciliation is possible. I hope his friends will never fail to impress upon him the ultimate gravity of the choices he has to make. I think he has the desire to choose rightly. The urgency is to make him see all that is involved in the nature of the right choice. The vital thing is his constant realisation that he battles with an enemy who never sleeps and will pay any price for victory.[16]

Walter Lippmann had meanwhile concluded that Roosevelt was not influenced by communism or fascism, but by his prejudices. The president, he wrote, possessed "the typical prejudices of the landed gentry, a love of the land and sympathy with agriculture—a distrust of new wealth based on enterprise or speculation, and of . . . the 'paper aristocracy'—a considerable tolerance for old landed property." Rooseveltian types, he wrote, also showed a sympathy "for the poor, plenty of courage, an aristocratic disdain of prudence—no great understanding of industry or finance, and a taste for the kind of civilized leisure of country life rather than for the restlessness of the big industrial and financial centers." The confusions and errors of the New Deal, he concluded, originated in its prejudices.[17]

The introduction of Roosevelt's "soak the wealthy" tax bill in Congress in late June 1935 and pressure for its immediate passage provoked a heated attack by Lippmann. This and other evidences of the president's instability led Lippmann to write a few weeks later that he had detected a change in Roosevelt's mood from "a collected leadership, prepared to compromise and then get on with recovery, to a distracted, episodic turning hither and thither" that could be disastrous. By insisting on "remote and minor issues" like the death sentence for holding companies in the public utilities bill, the president was showing no evidence of sound leadership, but rather resembled George Santayana's description of a fanatic, "that he redoubled his efforts when he had forgotten his aim."[18] For Roosevelt, however, Lippmann's criticism of his policies meant that the columnist "should come more into contact with the little fellow all over the country and see less of the big rich brother!"[19]

A few days later, Lippmann renewed his criticism of the president, writing that Roosevelt was acting in the summer of 1935 as if the same urgency existed as during the first few months of his presidency in 1933. Lippmann cautioned that those who acquired "extraordinary powers almost always find it hard to relinquish them," and Roosevelt had "reached a point in his career where, if he does not readjust his mind, he will become the victim of tempting delusions that invariably beset men who have played a great role on the world's stage." A month later Lippmann added that Roosevelt's recent disturbing actions had caused him to conclude "that the extraordinary powers intrusted to the President for meeting an emergency are being abused." He did not mean to imply, Lippmann wrote, that Roosevelt "has the ambitions of a dictator," but he did worry that the president had "let zeal, political calculation, the intoxication of power, heat and fatigue, confuse his grasp of a very simple, but very fundamental principle"—that in undertaking reforms there was "such a thing as due process, not merely in law, but in morals and in democratic methods."[20]

When Al Smith, the 1928 nominee of the Democrats for the presidency, broke with Roosevelt in 1936, Lippmann saw it as the result of the president's attempt to dominate the party and to purge it of all its Grover Cleveland and Al Smith elements. Roosevelt had done this in New York State, as governor, and he was now attempting to do it on a national scale. Roosevelt had, Lippmann wrote, "set out to do what no man has ever succeeded in doing in American politics, to make a national party not by compromise among factions but by personal domination," and in the process had become "more the agitator than the statesman."[21]

The undistributed profits tax bill that the New Deal sent to Congress in the 1936 session seemed confirmation for Lippmann of the prejudice against businessmen that he had described. Nobody was fooled by the administration's argument that the tax was required to replace revenue lost to the Treasury by the invalidation of the AAA by the Supreme Court earlier in the year. Lippmann rightly concluded that it was a reform and not a tax, an attempt "to force the distribution of [corporate] earnings by exacting a penalty if they are not distributed." The Roosevelt administration was "itself trying to regulate the dividend policy of corporations rather than to collect taxes justly." The bill he thought ill-considered and its implications not sufficiently thought out. It was a typical example, Lippmann wrote, of the New Deal's propensity "first to see a desirable objective, then to declare for it, then to legislate, then to study the problem; first you leap, then you look to see where you have landed."[22]

The Supreme Court's NRA decision in 1935, and a similar one on the AAA in January 1936, led to a rash of books on the court and on the constitution, which *TNR* found congenial liberals to review for its pages, and articles on the issues that were printed as well. In mid-1936, Bliven wrote progressive historian Charles Beard that he wished Beard to write an essay for *TNR* that would "give your judgment on what ought to be done about the issue of the Supreme Court and the Constitution. Should we have a new Constitutional amendment, and if so, what? Would it be possible for Congress to curb the powers of the Court by a simple legislative enactment? Should the size of the Court be increased and the bench packed with liberals, with the danger that in the future a conservative President might pack it with conservatives?"[23]

Nothing that the New Deal had done was enough to induce *TNR* to endorse Roosevelt for reelection in 1936. A balance sheet it drew up found far more liabilities in the New Deal than assets. Roosevelt, it charged, had given the impression of pleasing everybody, but had in fact done very little for anybody. Nor was *TNR* impressed with the man himself, whose intellectual capacities were now deemed so shallow that there was little common ground with intellectuals of the *TNR* variety. Moreover, as Seideman observed, "The horrifying spectacle of Mussolini and Hitler reinforced their fears of the cult of personality and *TNR*'s resolve to avoid becoming, as Bliven later boasted, a 'hero worshipper.'"[24] Here was clear confirmation of *TNR*'s awareness of the Rousseauvian direction FDR's conception of his role was taking.

But neither could *TNR* endorse FDR's Republican opponent, Governor Alf Landon of Kansas. It found the GOP candidate and platform trying to serve "two diametrically opposed purposes: first to hold all those who oppose the present administration, by vigorous denunciation of what it has done; second, to attract many of those who support the present administration by promising to do much the same things it has done—though by more efficient methods." The platform, *TNR* wrote, resembled "the wrapping on a patent-medicine bottle, advertised to cure everything at once, including high blood pressure and low blood pressure."[25]

When Lippmann announced his intention to vote for Landon in November, Bliven carped, "Mr. Lippmann's brilliant abilities are everywhere recognized and I do not doubt the sincerity of the mental processes that brought him to believe that Governor Landon, if elected, will do the same things as Mr. Roosevelt, only better." Bliven noted that the *New York Herald-Tribune* advertised Lippmann as "the man with the searchlight mind," and wrote that "it is the function of a searchlight to throw a dazzling illumination upon one small area, leaving everything else in darkness," which seemed to apply to Lippmann, who looked "at one small group of facts to the exclusion of others far more important," and needed to "soften his focus and extend his periphery."[26]

Even the Social Security Act of 1935 was considered inadequate by *The Nation* since it left so many workers uncovered by its provisions. In Kirchwey's view, no act at all was better than one so deficient as the one before Congress. An essay in that journal found the act's primary deficiency in the fact that it taxed the workers for their benefits, rather than laying the cost on higher income groups, an argument that Coyle would also make from his very different perspective. At the same time, the requirement that employers contribute an equal amount meant that their contribution would be passed on to consumers in the form of higher prices.[27] The worker would thus be taxed in two ways.

The Nation did, however, support the Wagner Labor Act with considerable enthusiasm, publishing numerous editorials calling for its passage. The act would, it pointed out, make possible "an ultimate shift in economic power from employers to workers." When the bill was passed, *The Nation*'s only criticism was of Roosevelt for not giving the bill more support when it was before Congress. It was not happy over the appearance given that the act was being forced on the president. A series of articles on Roosevelt by *The Nation*'s Washington correspondent, Paul Ward, in 1935, was harshly critical of the president, crediting him only with the Tennessee Valley Authority—"the best of the New Deal measures." Looking ahead to the 1936 presidential election, the journal editorialized that "Roosevelt, measured against what he might have been, cuts a far poorer figure than he will present next year in contrast with the choice of the Republican Party." Only by comparison with the GOP candidate, whomever he was, would Roosevelt stand out.[28] In another editorial, *The Nation* insisted that "we must have general principles, tested always by pragmatic action. A socialized future is the only adequate political solution for a mass-production world. To chart the specific American path to that future is our primary task." But unlike *TNR* it supported Roosevelt for reelection against any of the radical party candidates, arguing: "For the present, American radicalism must curb itself because it fears the uncertain future and because no new leadership has yet emerged." Yet Kirchwey, herself, voted for Norman Thomas.[29]

In March 1935, Pinchot mailed off to all members of Congress, to editors, bankers, and New Deal advisers, a letter opposing the Eccles-inspired Banking Act of 1935, arguing that the bill empowered an incumbent president seeking reelection "to use monetary power as a political weapon . . . [enabling] the leaders of the party to lower or raise the price-tag on everything the public owns or uses." He would be able "to check or promote a depression or a boom for political reasons," without reference to the public interest. Both in principle and practice, this is wrong.[30]

The following month Pinchot expressed concern over the vast discretionary powers that had been granted to Roosevelt by Congress, "more discretionary power than any ruler has had, in peace-time, in any constitional government."

I am more than sceptical about this kind of government. It is based on the exploded socialist and fascist idea that there can be found an all-wise and all-powerful personal leadership that will prove experienced enough and competent enough successfully to fix prices and wages, to regulate the amount of production, to decide which mergers shall be allowed and which forbidden, to approve or forbid monopoly, to encourage or condemn competition, and finally to control banking, money and credit, and to fix the price level and the size of the dollar. This, as it seems to me, is too big an order by a long shot.[31]

Later in the month Pinchot returned to the same theme with another letter on the bill. He was concerned, he wrote, with the effect that "placing vast, permissive and undefined powers in the President's hands, to be used at his discretion, will have, and, for that matter, is having, on business and farming and on the government itself." Those powers were found "in practically all the important bills that have come to Congress as administration measures," including the AAA, NIRA, relief bill, and the Eccles banking bill.

Taking the entire body of New Deal legislation together, and keeping in mind its permissive, in distinction to mandatory character, we have a picture of Congressional abdication on the one hand and executive usurpation on the other that is exceedingly disturbing.

Today almost everyone with property of any kind stands to a greater or less extent in awe of the government. For, by its newly forged personal and discretionary powers the Executive can withhold or extend financial help, and grant or deny immunity from the new laws and innumerable regulations. Banks, railroads, industrial and financial corporations fear the RFC. Farmers fear the AAA, even as they accept favors from it. Landlords, manufacturers, and business men fear the NRA. People who are involved in the wide-flung net of usually futile regimentation . . . and other people, who are dependent on the government's loaning agencies, hesitate to take a stand on public issues that may offend the administration. Organized labor, which is supposed to have gained by it, fears the NIRA, knowing that it can just as well be turned against as for it.

While Congress theoretically possessed the power to reclaim that which it had transferred to the White House, "with an executive possessed of a mammoth-sized pork barrel and supported by an incredible host of bureaucrats, Congress may find it a hard matter to come back." Moreover, "having patriotically disarmed itself during the crisis, Congress is as much afraid of the Executive as anyone." The New Deal had abandoned the Anglo-Saxon and American tradition of rights for that of communist Russia. Pinchot concluded, "Today, the nations of the world may be divided into two classes— the nations in which the government fears the people, and the nations in which the people fear the government. It is the New Deal's tragedy that it is moving this country into the second class."[32]

Probably no open letter that Pinchot penned during the New Deal years attracted as much attention and comment from liberals and conservatives alike as this one. Former Senator Robert Owen, now president of the National Monetary Conference, wrote that the New Deal Pinchot had described was "the fundamental doctrine of monarchy."[33] Ben Howe, chairman of New York City's Fusion Party was convinced that "not only is our Constitution now a scrap of paper, but that our liberties are gone beyond hope."[34] Conservative Paul Cravath found himself "more nearly in agreement with you than I would have expected." The "dictatorial powers" conferred upon Roosevelt were "un-American and dangerous."[35] The secretary of the Public Ownership League of America, whose members included Clarence Darrow, Paul Douglas, the LaFollettes, Floyd Olson, and others, wrote that he had "often thought along the very lines that you have mentioned. I have been much disturbed at some of the developments and trends in the present administration, but have hardly known what to make of it."[36]

Still committed to an inflationary solution to the depression, Pinchot wired Roosevelt and members of Congress in May 1935, in support of the inflationary Goldsborough amendment to the banking bill, arguing that it would "restore confidence, create business activity, cut down unemployment and relieve the government from the pressure that is driving it toward regimentation."[37] A month later he wrote Roosevelt of the uncertainty that existed in banking and real estate over dollar contracts and other obligations. Business and banking leaders had, he told FDR, finally changed their attitudes and "have now really begun to understand the value of your 1933 [inflationary] policy." Rumors that the administration was not supporting the Goldsborough amendment were, he told the President, "hurting you with the farmers in general, and with the cotton, wheat and tobacco raisers in particular. . . . Brandeis's opinion in the Frazier-Lemke bill case has centered the attention of the farm leaders on your money policy as their only dependable source of relief."[38]

To the editorial writer of the Manchester (Connecticut) *Record* Pinchot wrote: "I am glad you are fighting against fascism. For that's what the administration is, in effect, putting over on us. Of course, it is fascism with a string to it. But the string is getting weaker all the time."[39] The depression had lasted longer than necessary, he opined, "largely I think because Mr. Roosevelt has gone in for regimentation instead of monetary action like England's." He was hopeful that the Supreme Court's invalidation of the NRA would now lead Roosevelt to "realize the necessity of a more fundamental attack upon the American monetary problem."[40]

Pinchot pointed out to another correspondent that he had resigned as chairman of the People's League for Economic Security "because they went too far to the left." While Pinchot favored public ownership under some circumstances, he believed it should be only "to the extent that is necessary to prevent monopoly and protect competition. Here should be the definite limit. Everything else should be privately owned and run, and with the least possible government ownership and interference."[41] To liberal Senator William Borah he wrote:

The trouble with Roosevelt's advisors seems to be that they are moralists instead of economists. They are zealots, of rather inferior calibre, who, when once launched upon a plan of salvation, are willing to sacrifice almost everything and everybody in order to put their ism over. The messiah complex is a pretty dangerous thing, if divorced from common sense and humanity. And it is especially dangerous when it gets hold of men like Tugwell and Stuart Chase, who are not merely moralists but dramatic journalists, who never study anything long enough to understand its implications.

Pinchot hoped that the demonstrated failures of their policies would drive Roosevelt "back to his money policy of 1933. It's about all he's got left."[42]

By June 1935, Pinchot's disillusionment with Roosevelt and those around him seems to have become total. The administration's failure to support the inflationary Goldsborough amendment, even after the Supreme Court had rejected the NRA alternative, seemed to leave the New Deal with no recovery program at all. Pinchot wrote a fellow liberal that the president, "a much muddled man," had only two ways out of his impasse—"restoration of competition, and an intelligent money policy, including increase in the price of gold, and stabilization of the dollar's buying power."[43]

He was, he wrote another, "fast losing confidence in the President. . . . He seems to have no principles whatever, and no plan except the social worker exedients of his unworthy advisers, who are today mainly social worker moralists rather than economists or business men. The poor man has broken with one monetary adviser after another in a way that shows that he is casting for any stop gap expedient which seems, for the moment, to fill the need."

He had concluded it was useless to expect economic recovery from the Roosevelt administration and that the best hope was to work through the senate.[44] Roosevelt was "losing the respect of intelligent people" and "becoming the worst president we ever had:

After all, we are a business nation. And the idea that you help recovery by keeping business in a state of terror and uncertainty is a puerile one. If Roosevelt had said to himself, "I am going to smash up capitalism, and therefore will keep business in a condition of disorganization in which it dares not go ahead and do business," he would not, I think, have acted very differently.

He's out for just one thing now: votes. He probably figures he's gaining votes by moving to the left. But what talks most eloquently to even the poorest people is their chance of getting work and wages. And they are gradually sizing up Roosevelt as a tragic failure in this respect, though they still believe in his good will. I'm not so darned sure about his good will any more.[45]

From publisher Frank E. Gannet came the disturbing news that monetary policy was being left largely to Federal Reserve chair Marriner Eccles, a man who was "stupid on the [inflation] question and fundamentally unsound in his economic ideas. It is too bad. We must reach Eccles some way and educate him."[46] Pinchot responded that the administration's "soak the rich" tax proposal seemed to him "right enough, so far as its intentions and also its probable results are concerned," although he considered "the way it is being done is awfully bad." He told Gannett,

It seems to me that there is real danger that Roosevelt will slide us into a dictatorship yet.

It's significant that the opposition in Congress has been so weak, and that the Progessives are backing up the White House. Perhaps I am unduly alarmed. But I certainly am alarmed. I think the brain trust is out for blood, and it will sacrifice everything to holding on to power and putting its program over, no matter what kind of government this may lead us into.[47]

For Albert Shaw, editor of *Review of Reviews*, the problem was "that Frankfurter and his young men are forever snooping in and out behind the scenes, telling Roosevelt what to do and writing the laws Congress is ordered to enact."[48] This was a fairly common view of the New Deal procedure.

On 24 July 1935, newspapers reported that Amos Pinchot, a 1932 supporter of Roosevelt, had broken with the administration. As the *Chicago Tribune* put it: "Pinchot, for 25 years a leader in radical political thought, has written a letter to Prof. Felix Frankfurter, head of the Roosevelt brain trust, in which he pronounces the major policies of the administration 'ghastly and expensive failures.'" It quoted Pinchot's letter as having said, in part,

Roosevelt, with all his kindheartedness, is failing because he follows no consecutive line, and apparently doesn't think things through to the end.

Maybe I'm entirely wrong, but I've come to feel that the New Deal has not merely prolonged the depression but pretty thoroughly ditched for the time being the possibility of a constructive political and economic movement.

It has gathered under its wing a great many of the younger, liberal minded people who want to get in the game and be useful. And now it has left them in the blind alley of unworkable regimentation.

It has propagandized against democracy and built up an enormous bureaucratic executive power that always means inefficiency, extravagance, and dishonesty.

Most of you men in the brain trust are, I gather, of the opinion that capitalism and the profit motive are on their last legs. You believe, if I'm not mistaken, that competition is old fashioned and must yield to cooperation. That a brand new collectivist or Fascist order is around the corner, that a regimented, highly disciplined economy is the logical approach.

I can't agree with your hope, if it is your hope, that capitalism is moribund.

For his part, Pinchot believed that capitalism was a "tough old bird" that would outlive them all, and that "the profit system and competition . . . offer a far better chance for prosperity, freedom, happiness, individual progress, and a good standard of living than does socialism or Fascism." Business should be operated "with only such interference from the government as is necessary to provide equal opportunity and prevent monopoly." Roosevelt's actions had been so unpredictable that he was "the great uncertainty," thus "keeping a good many million men and women out of jobs.[49]

Within the Treasury Department, Herman Oliphant asked Morgenthau if he had read Pinchot's letter to Frankfurter, telling him that "everybody ought to read it. . . . He really said things to Felix."[50] Two weeks later Frankfurter had still not replied to the letter and Pinchot doubted that he would because he was "afraid his feelings are hurt." He added that "the New Dealers get rather peevish when their omniscience is questioned." Though Frankfurter was well-meaning, "he doesn't know his economics and has never thought very much about matters of this kind."[51] Nor did he think there was "a chance that Felix will be affected by my advice. He has the settlement worker's point of view. He is a fine, decent man, but he simply doesn't know anything about American business and its needs. After all, we are a business, industrial and farming country. And we've got to encourage production if we are to encourage re-employment."[52]

To another correspondent he wrote that Roosevelt's was "a sort of bogus liberalism, which prevents a realistic liberal movement, and yet accomplishes none of the ends which intelligent people are interested in." He continued:

Again, the emphasis of this administration, as I see it, is against capitalism, although he does not put this in words. The people who are most influential at Washington are, in effect, telling the country that capitalism has run its course, is unsound and unworkable, and that we must have a brand-new deal with collectivism as the goal.

I honestly don't believe Roosevelt is capable of thinking things out and sticking to any one course. Not merely has he no principles, but I can find no evidence that he has prejudices of a robust character. It seems to me that he has been a blank page upon which the New Dealers have written. They are a hodge-podge of collectivism and fascism. And I think the result is very unfortunate.[53]

Pinchot was appalled by the growing regimentation of agriculture under the AAA.

Mr. Tugwell restricts and regiments the planting of cotton on the ground there is too much of it. Thereupon the southern farmers plant peanuts. And, in turn, the New Deal restricts and regiments peanuts. The farmers then turn to potatoes. And Mr. Tugwell limits and regiments the planting of potatoes and makes it a crime to sell or buy any potatoes except those which the Department of Agriculture imagines to be required by the country.

The farmers will now turn, no doubt, to another crop, and that will be restricted and regimented, and so on, until the farms in the United States are managed in effect by a few men with little or no experience in farming or business. And I think we will have a more chaotic and destructive condition than has been known in the country. The only answer will be, from the administration's point of view, at least, for the government to take over the farms and abolish private farming. Which I think is exactly what Tugwell is heading for.[54]

Roosevelt had, Pinchot concluded, under Tugwell's influence, "gone into a perfectly crazy and destructive program of regulation, which can only complete itself by either collectivizing the farming industry or leaving it in private hands and regimenting every part of it by rigid fascist control." Only the Constitution and the Supreme Court stood between the United States and "the sort of business and agricultural regimentation which wrecked Italy." Of Roosevelt, he wrote, "Already Roosevelt has led the country into a trap, and we're getting more deeply involved in an unworkable managed economy every day. He is committing us in part to socialism and in part to fascism. I've lost respect for his intelligence. He is showing himself shallow and impatient-minded. A professed purist in politics, he uses to the full extent his patronage power. And he has built a steam roller in Congress that has proved just about irresistible so far."

Roosevelt was "trying to gain strength with the masses by a campaign of sheer bribery—getting people dependent on the government for everything, for wages, for loans, for living, for pay for their crops, mortgages, and so on." Roosevelt was "out to ride down the Constitution so that he can go on regimenting. Under the influence of the Tugwells, he is out to create a country of well-disciplined farmers, business men, and wage earners, who will come to heel promptly when the government blows its whistle."[55]

It all meant, Pinchot lamented, that the kind of liberal program he believed in had been delayed for at least ten years. He explained, "Anybody that talks about government ownership of railroads, pipe lines, or anything of the sort, is laughed at now on account of the discredit that Roosevelt has brought on government administration through the NRA, the AAA, and so on."

Pinchot had, he said, "gotten very much to dislike and distrust our friend in the White House. I think he is completely unprincipled and does good things or bad things purely as political opportunism suggests." Pinchot had decided to work in Borah's behalf for the Republican nomination in 1936, because he considered him "the only person who could beat Friendly Frank."[56] Justice Harlan Stone, agreed, he said, that "Roosevelt would go down in history as the foremost betrayer of the liberal movement in the United States."[57]

The New Deal was, Pinchot told pro-FDR publisher Roy Howard, "a bastard fascist collectivism." He told Howard, "Mr. Roosevelt, having kept the country in a state where millions of people can't make a go of things, comes along with his Christ-like charity and gives them, in the form of relief or benefits, a shabby little substitute for the good livelihood they might be making under an enlightened government. Of course he has to do this under the circumstances. But it's largely the fault of his policies that the rescue business is still required."[58]

The 1936 Republican Convention and its platform were, however, disappointments for Pinchot. The Resolutions Committee had formulated what he described as "a decent monetary plank," but were then "pulled off by Hoover and William Allen White."[59] But by now Pinchot was convinced that "any candidate and any party is preferable to Roosevelt at the head of so-called Democratic bureaucracy. Roosevelt is a dangerous, insincere demagogue. But what is more important, he is a dismal failure in the matter of recovery."[60]

A few weeks before the 1936 election, Pinchot addressed an open letter to his fellow long-time progressive, Secretary of the Interior Harold Ickes, setting out for him his reasons for not supporting Roosevelt again in 1936. He told Ickes,

The truth is that Mr. Roosevelt has followed a course which has made many sincere, liberal-minded people, who voted for him in 1932, believe that a radical change has taken place in his thinking. Today they sense in the President a growing distrust of American ways of life. More than that, they are beginning to suspect that he would not be sorry to see this country turn toward an economic and political order of a very different kind. In a word, they are asking, in all honesty, whether at heart Mr. Roosevelt is a liberal or a socialist. . . . I think the change in his attitude, in his philosophy, political and economic, since 1932, is perhaps the most important single issue in this campaign.

If Mr. Roosevelt is returned to power, his own philosophy and that of his advisors will drive him forward with his plan for a managed and highly disciplined America. And when this plan fails, as I think it is bound to, he will be forced, in order to delay its total collapse, to go in for more and more management, more and more discipline, and increasingly rigorous socialist forms of control.

Four years of the New Deal had left the United States with "eleven millions unemployed, twenty millions on relief." Roosevelt had "unwisely and consistently discouraged production, both on the farm and in the factory, although production is the one major force that can bring back recovery, employment and good times." The failure to recover had resulted from the fact that "the President, on bad advice, has played cat and mouse with business for three years." The New Deal would go down in history "not merely as an economic and political failure, but as a betrayal of American progress."[61]

A socialist friend, Reverend John Haynes Holmes of New York City, wrote Pinchot that they seemed

to be in absolute agreement on the matter of the President as a personality. I long since lost all confidence in his political integrity. He is essentially a play-boy and not a serious leader. His work is that of improvisation, not of statesmanship. He is a grand amateur yachtsman, having a perfectly glorious time with his sport of sailing, but is not in any sense of the word a sea captain seriously engaged in the business of navigating a great ship through storms and shoals to a safe harbor. I hate to say it, but I have long since learned not to trust him, therefore could never in any sense of the word surrender myself to his guidance. I tremble for the nation when I think that its destiny is in his hands.[62]

Industrialist Ralph Flanders wrote that Roosevelt's "intentions are of the best, but he simply doesn't know what is going on about him or what he himself is doing."[63] Another correspondent wrote that FDR had "been 'sold' the Marxian class philosophy. Had he been as familiar with the class-war doctrine as you and I are, he would have had no difficulty in discerning the underlying principles of the New Deal. They put one over on him and he swallowed it as something new and original."[64]

But Pinchot's letter attracted criticism from some liberals, including Edgar Cook, chairman of the Progessive Republican Voters League for Roosevelt, in which Pinchot had been a featured name in 1932.[65] While Ickes responded with a sarcastic letter to Pinchot, he wrote to Felix Frankfurter that Pinchot's defection from FDR was "pitiable." "I have seen so many progressives fall by the wayside during the course of a long life that I have to take these distressing events as a matter of course. I must confess, however, that Amos Pinchot's defection gave me a little extra pang."[66]

— 5 —

Creative Economics

David Cushman Coyle returned to a recurrent theme in an article for the *National Conference of Social Work* on "Necessary Changes of Opinion in the New Social Order," writing, "Our environment has changed with a vengeance." The main cause of unemployment, he repeated, was the collapse of the service industries, which had prospered in the 1920s. The service industries were primarily luxuries, and expenditures on luxuries were the first casualty in hard times. "Society," he wrote, "will have to develop means for stabilizing the market for services. Old values, old judgments, and old maxims that interfere with the necessary stabilizing of the market for services cannot survive the coming of the age of plenty." What was required was that the "distribution of income through over-investment and the building of debt . . . become a small item, and the distribution of income through income taxes and through contributions to the social services stimulated by tax exemptions . . . become a very large item." In short, surplus income would have to be diverted from investment and circulated through spending.

In order to stimulate such spending, consumers must be relieved of the sales taxes, tariffs, and public-service charges that drained away their purchasing power. Their place would be taken by "heavy income taxes on the upper brackets, with large exemptions for contributions to semipublic institutions . . . [and] heavy taxation of undistributed corporate surpluses, to force corporation income into dividends and wages." "Communism," Coyle conceded, "is one way of providing for the necessary distribution and allocation of income. The control of the flow of money by the tax system is the other way. . . . At the present time the American people are not willing to try communism. Whether communism is adapted to the American temperament is very doubtful."

The successful "passage into the new age of plenty will depend on whether the public can be led to agree to the necessary measures for distributing purchasing power and for allocating surplus to spending for services." An essential measure would be "old age pensions," which must "come to be regarded not as a dole to the destitute, but as a universal right." Such pensions would create "a class of buyers who have nothing to sell . . . encourage retirement and make more room for the younger workers, and above all . . . will remove the necessity of the pathetic and hopeless efforts to lay by investments for old age." Other plans for "guaranteeing personal security" would also have a place, such as "accident and sickness insurance," to remove the "desperate pressure to save and invest and lose money." Since too much investment was a "poison," the provision of economic security was "not only a moral obligation resting on society, but it is a technical necessity for the operation of the age of plenty. Basic security is the prerequisite for that habit of spending and not saving that the age of plenty demands."

Government might impose control over "working hours and a moderate minimum wage," without destroying the freedom of business, but control of production and prices destroyed business elasticity and "restrictions on freedom tend to become very severe." The "genius" of the American people "for not obeying superfluous laws is immense," he pointed out, and there was "no widespread desire in America for any neatly organized society" at the expense of "freedom of individual action."

Coyle then disposed of the collectivist mood of the new liberals, writing that

public opinion, and especially liberal opinion, has by the existing preponderance of the economic crisis been led into a false perspective. We have temporarily overlooked the fact that in the new social order manufacturing will be a minor activity; that the service industries will be the dominant half of the economic system; and that the growth of our culture demands freedom of experimentation in the field of services. In the long run a planned economic order is not the central focus of an adequately planned society for an age of plenty. . . . If a satisfactory adjustment to the age of plenty is to be attained, it is vitally important to plan for the preservation of the largest possible freedom of variation, of experimentation, and of adventure. . . . The civilization now beginning will not be invested and imposed by a dictator; it will develop out of the reactions of all the people to the conditions of their life and to the sporadic contributions of genius.

Coyle told social workers the following:

You have struggled for years to establish the decencies of life for their own sake. The time has now come when you can demand the means for an expanded social-work program in the name of economic law. The fates have taken your side. The heavy artillery has come up—in fact it is parked in the White House.[1]

In December 1933, Coyle published an article in the *Atlantic Monthly* in which he examined the promise he saw for the economy in an expanded public works program. Prosperity had always been driven by some new industry, most recently by the automobile. That industry had furnished employment for many people, both directly and indirectly. "Where," Coyle asked, "did all the money come from to pay the wages in all of these new jobs?" He answered, "Out of the pockets of people who were spending more money on the car than they used to spend on the family bicycles. Surplus income, instead of being saved, was being spent on worldly pleasure. Benjamin Franklin's bones rolled over in his grave, but the national income rose by leaps and bounds. The new toy was making the American spend more money, so the American people were getting more money to spend—for every time one person spent a dollar someone else got it." But in the late 1920s, Coyle observed, Americans had begun to pay more attention to bond salesmen than to automobile salesmen, with the result that money was drained away from spending and into savings. Far from being a period of extravagance, as was frequently charged, the boom years were a period of "unprecedented thrift. Never in history did any people 'save' such a lot of money or 'invest' their savings in such a magnificent array of cats and dogs." Business had collapsed under the burden of the colossal amount of debt thus accumulated.

If America were now to recover from the depression, it needed "a new industry that will make us start spending again, and one that will not lead us into the fatal paths of 'investment.'" Contrary to the cries of orthodox economists, bankers, and businessmen, the last thing the nation needed was a revival of the capital goods industry, which would only recreate the conditions that had produced the crash and depression. Public works offered the promise of being the new industry that could furnish employment and create the buying power that would not be diverted into savings and investment. "The real function of federal spending," Coyle wrote, "is not to furnish extra buying power out of hat, but to turn surplus income back into buying power while preventing surplus income from getting into excessive investment. Its effectiveness, therefore, depended upon taxation of surplus income." In the Age of Plenty "a large part of the surplus income will be spent by the people themselves on their own personal activities." This could only be done, however, after a "universal guarantee of basic economic security for all members of the social body, quite regardless of age, color, or previous condition of economic ineptitude." This would include "free education, free public health services, accident and unemployment insurance, and, above all, a generous old-age pension system. With such a system in place, the people would "dare to spend their incomes, and when the people dare to spend their incomes the Age of Plenty will really be at hand."

By supporting federal control of concentrated industries, Coyle was close to the position of the planners within the Roosevelt administration, and he initially supported the National Industrial Recovery Act. It would, he wrote, be a start on the road to recovery, but after it had "done all that can be done with shorter hours and higher wages, the public works program must take hold and carry on from that point." But he also initially viewed the NRA as the blueprint for a new industrial policy that would "turn surplus income into buying power without forcing it to pass through the classic sequence of hope, investment, bankruptcy and disgust." Coyle would not always be so complimentary of the NRA.[2]

By the end of 1933 Coyle had clearly become something of a New Deal insider, held in high esteem by those who continued to adhere to Brandeisian views of the economy. As Arthur Schlesinger, Jr. has written, "Corcoran and Cohen, like Brandeis and Frankfurter, were working mainly behind the scenes. Moreover, all four men, as lawyers, were more inclined to respond to specific cases than to develop a general rationale. Accordingly, the most rounded presentation of the Brandeis position in 1935 came from a nonlawyer outside government, David Cushman Coyle."[3] Of course, Coyle was not outside government, nor did his "presentation of the Brandeis position" begin in 1935. It had begun in 1932.

In an America whose liberal tradition seemed to have lost its traditional moorings and to have embraced an anticapitalist ideology that threatened not only economic, but also political freedom,

Coyle stood out as a defender of free enterprise, somewhere between the collectivists and traditional liberals. Moreover, his defense embraced a novel and comprehensive view of the economy
that set him apart from other defenders of traditional liberalism
who were easily dismissed by collectivist liberals as mere defenders
of the status quo. Far from being merely a Brandeisian, Coyle inte-
grated Brandeisian ideas into a far more comprehensive and intel-
ligible theory that Brandeisians could support even while it gave
their proposed reforms to the economy a more rigorous rationale.

Thus, when a Marxist, Mary van Kleeck, attacked the New Deal
in a speech before the National Conference of Social Work to an
enthusiastic response, it was Coyle, says Schlesinger, who "was
quickly summoned to reply," which he did with a "powerful piece"
for *Survey* magazine.[4] In his article, Coyle drew a contrast between
what he described as "engineering planning" and "policy planning."
The former, he wrote, was appropriate for projects like the Panama
Canal, where a blueprint was followed and full regimentation was
required without provision for personal liberty. "The problem of
discipline," he wrote, "is met by the power to hire and fire, that is,
it depends on a reserve of labor outside the plan." But, he explained,

If an engineering plan were to be applied to the nation as a whole, the
necessary discipline would depend on the death penalty, since those who
have unstandardized minds cannot be fired anywhere except into the next
world. Our nearest approach to a general engineering plan are our traffic
laws, backed by a staggering annual death-toll. . . . These limitations of
the engineering type of planning are sometimes overlooked by people who
are not engineers by profession.

Policy planning, on the other hand, had a long and successful
tradition in the United States, dating back to the imposition of high
tariff policies at the insistence of Alexander Hamilton. Their purpose had been to "cause money to flow from the consumer and farmer
into the hands of the financier," in order "to cause the building of
factories to free us from dependence on England." Policy planning
had also made possible the acqusition of the western territories,
and the land given to railroads, homesteaders, and schools.

There is always danger that we may adopt measures that will require too
strict a discipline of too large a number of citizens. Prohibition was an
example and NRA shows signs of being another. These were national plans
of the engineering or operational type, and in the absence of an enforce-
able death penalty, they had small chance of success. The people have a
technique for throwing off discipline of this kind. The lesson is plain that

national planning of the operation of industry, while practicable and necessary in certain limited centralized activities such as power and oil, is not technically suitable for general application to the nation as a whole.

Absent the consent of the governed, engineering planning could be achieved only through revolution. But Coyle warned that after the initial elation, "the long struggle settles down again with new wrongs, new intolerance of reason, new horrors." The new social order should be established without it. The conflict in America for the foreseeable future, Coyle argued, was between, on the one side, "all those who get their living by producing, distributing and selling goods and service: farmers, miners, laborers, the professions and the owners and operators of business and industry." The other side, a decided minority, consisted of "those who get their living by producing, distributing and selling securities, so called, and the paper that stands for speculation in commodities, capital goods and land." He explained, "Our highly productive economic system cannot be operated under the control of those who deal in paper values. . . . Industry and labor can fight over the red ink, but neither can survive unless the power of Finance is destroyed. High Finance must be reduced to an humble servant of production before this nation can have stable prosperity."

Finance possessed money, but the people had votes, and if "the people decide to tax away the power of Finance, there is no effective way of resistance." It was vital to define the issue in such a way as to win the support of the middle class rather than to drive them into the arms of the enemy.

Coyle wrote, "Before the crash of 1929 the main fortress of the status quo stood impregnable, the power of high Finance was mighty in the earth." And big finance still had the "power to deceive the people, to finance great waves of propaganda, to buy elections, evade laws, corrupt governments. The battle is no easy victory, but a dirty, heartbreaking struggle." The battle, he insisted, was not between the New Deal and communism, but rather between the New Deal and the powers of finance: "If we fail, the financial powers will sweep back in a fascist revolution. They will attempt to run the economic system by the same principles that wrecked it in 1929 but with every avenue of criticism blocked and every safety valve wired down. What will happen when their boiler explodes again is not pleasant to think about. We had better win this fight now while we have a chance."[5]

After a year and a half of the New Deal, Coyle was convinced that the most important progress shown was that toward "an understanding of the problem of new investment." Initially, he wrote, the New Deal seemed to have proceeded in agreement with the views of orthodox economists "that recovery from the existing depression would of course come in a pattern similar to previous recoveries, that is, by a revival of long-term capital investment," and much of the Roosevelt program had been "more or less definitely colored by this underlying assumption." He continued,

The radicals, of course, had an easy solution right at hand. By abolishing the system of private ownership in business, the Government could relieve itself at once of the bankers and all their works. . . . [But] the recognized experts advised that "confidence" had to be restored, and the Government would have been absurd not to take the best advice that was to be had. The advice happened to be wrong, but that was just what one has to expect in the earlier stages of a period of transition.

The NRA, Coyle concluded, had failed in its goal to increase consumer purchasing power by forcing businesses to pay higher wages, because "the missing buying power is not in the hands of employers as a class, but in the hands of a different class that cuts across the category of employers and employees." Much of it was "in the hands of those who have more money than they can or will spend, whether they be corporation executives or stockholders or movie stars or successful kidnappers or unusually fortunate landlords." The NRA's attempts to plan, he wrote, had created more problems than they solved. Meanwhile, he found growing awareness within the New Deal that prosperity could not come through the orthodox means of "new capital investment," and that, on the contrary, "Wall Street must be curbed before prosperity can be made safe business. . . . Events are shaping that will blow away the fog from the minds of the experts and of the people, leaving the New Deal face to face with public enemy number one, the power of high finance."

The essence of the New Deal is that some day the lines shall be drawn for a battle between the American people and the Lords of Finance. Everything that interferes with the coming of the Day and the drawing of that battle line is an obstacle to the New Deal. . . . The New Deal is a liberal revolution against the disastrous rule of high finance, and its relation to labor and to radicalism needs to be kept clear. If high finance can be destroyed by the middle class, with the help of labor votes, the national income will be greatly increased, and opportunities for employment will be numerous. . . . In this sense, therefore, labor can fairly be asked to postpone its demands until better times. From the radical viewpoint, however, the case is quite different. Labor, in the radical sense, does not want higher wages, shorter hours, and collective bargaining, but the destruction of private business. A liberal revolution that will provide security and a high standard of living without destroying private business is repugnant to radical ideas.

An awareness of the undesirability of new investment had even begun to penetrate the business world, Coyle observed, as the NRA code authorities for the various industries had become "sensitive to the unpleasant effect of new competition that might appear in their fields if new capital plant were to be constructed. They feel a vested interest in excluding new equipment while the existing equipment is running at less than capacity." Coyle added,

But without a large volume of new investment, how can the New Deal bring on prosperity and find jobs at good wages for ten million surplus men? . . . In its simplest form the program is to build public works and charge the bill to surplus funds through the income and inheritance tax. . . . In practice the Public Works program has a limited usefulness. . . . The most practicable line of attack appears to be through the measures of economic security—old-age pensions and various kinds of insurance. If these measures can be adopted on a scale that will affect moderate-sized incomes, the total volume of savings will be reduced definitely, and the problem of redistribution will be partly relieved. . . . The habit of corporate saving will need to be broken up by taxation of undistributed profits. The prevention of Wall Street, or "sound money," inflation will need to be buttressed by a sufficient control of the banks to make them expand and contract short-time loans as directed. Whether public ownership of the banks is necessary remains to be seen. In any case there can be no doubt that bankers will in future play the game as they are told, or else.[6]

In a July 1935 article for the *Virginia Quarterly Review*, Coyle espoused a very Brandeisian position in appealing for the decentralization of industry. He wrote, "The illness of capitalism, from which our radical friends derive such keen satisfaction, is closely connected with the tendency of capitalism to run to extreme centralization. . . . If the American people want to avoid communism, they will have to tackle capitalism and force it to decentralize." Centralization led to control of big business by big finance, with all its attendant abuses, and also to the price fixing that was inimical to a free economy. Some businesses, by their nature, were inevitably centralized and price fixed, and must eventually be taken over by the government. Railroads, he wrote, were "already far along" toward that state, while electric power was moving rapidly toward it. The war was already on, and Coyle described the progress so far achieved under the New Deal. There were the first securities act; the attack by the administration and Congress on the power holding companies—the "citadel of high finance"; social security, which would "reduce the hopeless and pathetic effort to save against a rainy day, and thus cut off from financiers their customary supply of lambs." Next, heavy income and inheritance taxes would "destroy the financial group itself," and federal control of bank credit seemed on its way in the Eccles banking bill. Ahead were prospects of graduated corporate taxes and levies on corporate undivided profits. All were weapons in the war against finance, and there would "be no peace till high finance is destroyed."[7]

The month after the article appeared, veteran progressive Norman Hapgood wrote to Louis Brandeis:

In a letter to me about the Virginia Quarterly article Coyle writes: "Rex Tugwell read the article and told me he had never read anything with which he disagreed so completely. Jerry [Jerome] Frank, who was present, said, 'for gosh sake, Dave, you haven't gone Brandeis, have you?' and I told him, 'hell, I've always been Brandeis. . . .' The big battle is coming on, and them that is here will have the fun.[8]

Reference to conflict within the New Deal was not uncommon. In early February 1934, Coyle declined a dinner invitation from Judge Louis Brandeis, explaining that he had "a previous engagement with Mr. Eccles of the Treasury, whom I've never met and who may be an important help to our side." He added that he hoped Brandeis would excuse his violation of etiquette, but "war is war, and in my simple way I'm taking this war seriously."[9] Coyle found in Eccles a kindred soul whose views were in many ways a mirror of his own.[10]

Two weeks before the 1934 congressional elections a Felix Morley editorial excoriated the New Deal for "debauching politics," writing, "Few more pernicious influences ever enter into politics than the use of Government expenditures as bait to catch votes." It represented "a bankruptcy of statesmanship over which the country may well be deeply concerned."[11] A few days later the *Post* returned to the theme with an editorial that attacked a memorandum to Democratic candidates from Emil Hurja of the Democratic National Committee describing federal relief expenditures for various states. It wondered if the lavish relief expenditures were "permitted partly in order to buy Democratic votes?"[12] If not, what was the point of the memorandum?

Ever hopeful, Walter Lippmann found in Roosevelt's 1935 state of the union address evidence that the president intended to move away from the regimentation of the NRA and the AAA and toward an emphasis, instead, to "supplement and correct, to stimulate and balance the operation of private enterprise." It was the duty of the government, he wrote, to abandon "merely punitive and terroristic attacks on private business and banking in favor of direct regulation of specific evils."[13] Lippmann summed up his position soon after the second anniversary of the New Deal, when he responded to a Frank Kent column that had been critical of FDR and the New Deal a few days earlier. Lippmann pointed out that he, too, had disagreed "with some of the major policies and much of the strategy of the New Deal," but he wished the president well "in what I take to be his effort to preserve the essentials of a free social order in the midst of a world-wide upheaval." Two years yet remained of Roosevelt's term in office and it was imperative that "Americans should pass through those two years with courage and confidence in their institutions and trust in the nation's strength." Critics served no useful purpose if they destroyed "the only man who can be President during those two years, and they must not seek to paralyze the government by confusing the duty of criticism with irreconcilable enmity and partisanship."[14]

Kent responded a few days later with a column in which he wrote that "all the Lippmann subtlety cannot alter the fact" that the New Deal had failed to produce recovery, despite its enormous expenditures and unlimited authority. Kent pointed out that "more than one-sixth of the nation is living on relief, where, both in numbers and in cost, peaks not dreamed of a year ago have been reached." This was naturally distressing for Lippmann, he wrote, since he had "early embraced the New Deal with such soulful enthusiasm" and was now "distinctly unhappy" that it was "losing public support and crumbling before his eyes." It was typical of New Dealers, Kent wrote, to ascribe unworthy personal motives to its critics, but it was unpleasant to see Lippmann joining in the position that "failure to support Mr. Roosevelt is lese majeste."[15]

On the second anniversary of the New Deal, Morley wrote that it found "the weaknesses of the Administration dominant. Since the defeat of the World Court Resolution the President's loss of leadership has become increasingly apparent and in the whole Work-Relief Bill fiasco he shows up very badly. He wrote, "Roosevelt seems completely lacking in coordinating power. He is good on initiation—very poor on correlation." The New Deal was "running down rapidly. Trying to please almost everybody it is steadily increasing suspicion of the reality of its programs, without producing constructive results—except dangerously rising food prices—to stave off opposition. But no alternatives crystallize. The old-school Republicans are finished . . . and the new school not yet organized."[16] But a few weeks later, Morley was more optimstic, noting that the "Republican movement to cut the tap roots to Wall Street and reorganize under Lincolnesque, mid-western leadership is growing. Dave Hinshaw [progressive Republican] was in to sound me out the other day. William Allen White [progressive Republican] is a powerful man in the councils, & if they can offer anything positive it may be hard for F.D.R. in '36. He is fishing off Florida—& his prestige is decidedly waning."[17]

Morley had mixed feelings about the Supreme Court decisions of 27 May 1935. Listing the verdict against the NRA, the Frazier–Lemke farm bankruptcy act, and Roosevelt's removal of the late William E. Humphrey as federal trade commissioner, Morley wrote in his journal that it was "by far the heaviest blow yet dealt the New Deal." The decisions had struck "at the exercise of executive dictation, at over-expansion of the legislative prerogative, and at excessive delegation of power by the legislature to the executive. Thus the road to the development of Fascism is blocked—and a big stimulus given to movements for Constitutional revision." The NRA decision had "pretty well shot the Roosevelt program, for it is sure to raise the question of constitutionality in a number of allied fields. But it is quite arguable that the disciplinary effect, in what has been a highly inchoate and haphazard program, will in the long run be all to the good." Morley added, "No real liberal, however he may dislike Big Business, can favor the distinct drift towards Fascism which has been so perceptible in late months."[18]

In an editorial a couple of days later, Morley wrote that the decision in the NRA case had "built an insurmountable barrier to any . . . drift toward dictatorship in the United States." He continued:

Of course no reasonable observer has ever visualized Mr. Roosevelt as having the slightest desire to wield the scepter of tyranny. On the other hand there can be few discerning Americans who have failed to notice the tacit encouragement which some New Deal measures have given to assaults upon the basic structure of our government. What is the fundamental reason for the feverish, if transient, reception accorded to Upton Sinclair, Dr. Townsend, Huey Long, Father Coughlin and lesser-known rabble-rousers? Simply that the present Administration has whetted the appetite of the unthinking by intimating that wishes may become horses if the orderly processes of the Federal system are broken down to centralize power in the hands of an omnipotent executive.

The Supreme Court decision should fortify Roosevelt "against the vicious attacks of demagogues and the ill-advised promptings of irresponsible friends."[19]

A few days later, when Roosevelt struck out at the Supreme Court in a press conference, charging that it had taken a "horse and buggy" view of the commerce clause of the Constitution, Morley wrote an editorial for the *Post* captioned "A President Leaves His Party," in which he noted that FDR and the New Dealers had come out "frankly for permanent centralization and against the Jeffersonian tradition of State's rights." In his journal, Morley wrote that he was squarely opposed to Roosevelt over the issue: "The United States is too huge and varied for the form of centralization which he seems to desire; it is not yet sufficiently advanced in the technique of government or the elements of the merit system to promise successful socialization even if it were theoretically desirable." The court's decision stood "out as a dam against the general tendency of the times."[20]

Like many other traditional liberals, Morley was disturbed by the President's emergency tax bill, and his efforts to ram it through Congress during the 1935 session. Roosevelt, he confided to his journal, had gotten "into a frightful muddle on his tax program." Like other traditional liberals, Morley sympathized with the bill more than the method, writing, "Of course the income tax base will have to be greatly broadened, in addition to 'soak-the-rich' endeavors, if revenue is even to begin to catch up with expenditures." Morever, Morley confessed to "a certain sympathy with the plan to scale up the rates on corporation profits," even though he admitted it was unfair, because there was "something to be said for the Brandeis theory of 'pulverization' if the virtues of Democracy are to be preserved." At the same time, however, it seemed to represent "a reversion to the 'horse and buggy' era which makes the President's indorsement as inconsistent as many of his other positions." Fortunately, Morley foresaw FDR's failure to ram the legislation through Congress without debate or amendment.[21]

In an editorial the following month, Morley wrote that instead of fulfilling his responsibility "to lead the country toward sound and practical objectives," Roosevelt was instead relying on "appeals to whims and prejudices which he believes to be popular at the moment." An example was Roosevelt's tax program, a "punitive measure" designed to appeal to "a vindictive element in the population" that could only delay recovery by discouraging private enterprise.[22] After Congress adjourned in August 1935, Morley called for "virile leadership" in an editorial, writing that it was not shown by "imposing a mass of uncoordinated measures upon a people who to a very large extent have little or no understanding of their underlying implications," nor in "seducing great groups of voters by offering them 57 varieties of government subventions." Now, Morley wrote, was Roosevelt's opportunity "to reflect upon the value of the American tradition, while there is still time to save its essential virtues from irredeemable decay."[23]

In August 1935 Morley took aim at the "botchery" in unemployment relief, editorializing that it had been "placed in the hands of narrowly trained social workers who have thoroughly emphasized what is ethical at the expense of what is practical." The "maze" of New Deal agencies were filled with "wild confusion," and an "utter absence of coordination," which, despite the expenditure of billions of dollars had "utterly failed to produce any real improvement in employment."[24]

Although Congress had given Roosevelt carte blanche in turning over to him the huge $4.8 billion work relief appropriation, it had written a number of recommendations into the bill for the spending of the money, many of which called for substantial projects that might stimulate recovery. Instead, Roosevelt had virtually ignored the recommendations in the bill and was using it for work relief. Morley wondered if Congress would have been so quick to pass the appropriation had they known that almost all of the money would be spent for "park puttering, futile research by inexpert 'white collar' workers and trifling repair jobs."[25]

In September 1935, Morley examined the state of liberal thought, and wrote that he was "becoming increasingly impatient with the superificial quality of radical thought." While it had been attractive to him at an earlier period in his life, he now found its "emotionalized watery content" irritated him "where it does not antagonize me." He added that "the Liberal viewpoint is today more menaced from the left than from the right. To survive Liberalism must become a fighting creed, its sword sharpened and tempered by superior intellectual quality. To that task my full energies are now devoted."[26]

When, a few days later, Roosevelt announced a breathing spell from the onslaught of New Deal legislation in a letter to publisher Roy Howard, Morley saw it as an opportunity for the president "to regain some of the ground he is now rapidly losing," but Morley added that "more and more he gives the impression of being thoroughly untrustworthy, in spite of fair words."[27]

In November, as he looked ahead to the presidential election a year in the offing, Morley wrote that it appeared "in spite of his intellectual shallowness and many grievous errors," Roosevelt would likely be reelected, in part because the Republican Party was moribund, and in part because FDR seemed to have "a sort of sixth sense which keeps him in the current of the Weltanschaung no matter how drifting and erratic his course."[28] And a few days later Morley wrote that it was "increasingly difficult . . . to see how support for the New Deal and real Liberalism can be regarded as synonymous, in view of such revelations as the fact that Tugwell, in the R[esettlement] A[dministration] 'has hired 12,089 persons to provide jobs for only 5,072 relief workers,' as the N.Y. Times puts it this morning."[29]

A few days later Morley took up in an editorial Lewis Douglas's statement that, in Morley's words, "our relatively exclusive income tax encourages—or at least fails to check—loose spending." Morley wrote:

Great Britain, Mr. Douglas points out, has about 2,000,000 unemployed and from 3,000,000 to 4,000,000 income tax payers. The inference is, of course, that the influence of taxpayers upon the budget is more cogent than that of jobless men. At any rate, the British government has followed a policy of thrift and economy without inflicting any undue hardship upon the unemployed.

In the United States the situation is quite the reverse. We have approximately 10,000,000 men out of work and fewer than 2,000,000 income tax payers contributing revenue to the Federal Treasury. The major difference lies in the exempting of moderate incomes in this country from taxation. Not only does that practice deny the Government much-needed revenue, but it also greatly reduces the pressure that would otherwise be brought to bear upon Congress to curtail its spending habits.[30]

When the Supreme Court invalidated the Agriculture Adjustment Act in January 1936, Morley wrote that it was "a staggering blow for Roosevelt and not less so because it foreshadows even further defeats for the New Deal. I hope Social Security may be saved from the wrecking. Unless he sponsors a Constitutional Amendment I cannot see what his election program will be." After Roosevelt's Jackson Day speech, that Morley described as "a vituperative, rabble-rousing but essentially thin effort," he wrote that the president's "chief purpose now seems to be to inflame the mob against largely imaginary enemies—a dangerous and wicked course of action at a time like this."[31]

Roosevelt's speeches continued to distress Morley and to conflict with his notion of liberalism. One day in late April he inspired a *Post* editorial. Roosevelt had outlined a philosophy of government that could reasonably be characterized as "simple, yet eternally false." His speech had shown "that the Administration has been proceeding backward, not as an emergency policy, not to get around a temporary impasse, but to fulfill what the President calls 'my economic and social philosophy, and incidentally, my political philosophy as well.'" Roosevelt had avoided mention of "the rapid strides toward recovery made during the past three years by depressed countries that have not had recourse to price-raising and controlled production plans," and he had also avoided "the one question upper most in the minds of everyone. That is, why, in view of all the wonderful things that he claims to have accomplished, are so many Americans still unemployed."[32]

Looking at the Republican Convention in June 1936, Morley editorialized that the Roosevelt administration's attempts to bring about recovery by setting up "'new instrumentalities of power' in Washington [in] flagrant disregard of constitutional restrictions upon Federal power" had utterly transformed the respective positions of the two parties, causing the Republican Party to replace the Democrats as the defender of states' rights. With the trend "toward the exercise of dictatorial powers in Washington, it is not essentially inconsistent for the GOP to become the champion of States' rights," but rather a matter of "preserving the balance of governmental authority—of upholding the American system."[33]

In late June he confided to his journal that Roosevelt's acceptance speech at the Philadelphia convention had caused him to worry that "that the position the President is taking may do more to destroy than to save democracy. There is no doubt of the intensity of the man's feelings—whether induced by self-hypnoses or otherwise—but there is very good reason to suspect his competence. . . . It begins to look as though he is that dangerous type of megalomaniac who is totally without sense either of proportion or of his own deficiencies." From Roosevelt's remarks he seemed determined "to destroy big business or perhaps even the capitalist system itself," with "little or no enlightenment as to what he plans to substitite for that which he will tear down." Morley added:

His really alarming speech closes the emotional orgy of the Philadelphia Convention, from which I returned on Thursday afternoon, after an interesting three-day stay. The simulated passion of the speakers and the stimulated passions of the mob there were thought-provoking. Even without the constant reiteration of the phrase "our leader"—Mein Fuhrer—it would have been easy to discern the way the tides are flowing. His election is very clearly going to be a fight for the preservation of American institutions, for if once the established safeguards against dictatorship are broken down personal rule would be sure to follow. . . . The whole circus atmosphere at Philadelphia became highly offensive. And I cannot myself see any hope for the country in a party which so panders to ignorance and emotion, while relying on the twin evils of patronage and subsidies to hold its discordant elements together.[34]

In late July Morley looked at the presidential campaign and confided to his journal,

The issue at hand is to keep Democracy functioning, and the liberal spirit alive, in this country. For this objective I cannot help believing that Landon . . . is a far more reliable man than Roosevelt. For all of the latter's humanitarianism his line of progressive centralization is one which paves the way towards State Socialism. And State Socialism in this country means Fascism, as the Coughlin–Townsend–Smith–Lemke movement amply indicates. Amorphous as is this "Revolt of the Masses" it is politically dangerous, and bitterly as it now opposes Roosevelt, he has paved the way for it.[35]

— 6 —

Collectivists and the Court

The publication of Harold Laski's book, *The Rise of Liberalism*, caused Felix Morley to read it and to write a review of it for the Post. In his journal, Morley wrote that the book was "very striking," in the way Laski had tried to show that "Liberalism, as the philosophy of a business civilization, is played out." Morley agreed that capitalism was very much on the defensive, but he remained confident of its vitality in America under the right leadership, even if Roosevelt were reelected.[1]

In his published review Morley wrote that although *The Rise of Liberalism* was not about the United States, its content and conclusions were important for Americans because Laski's "influence on the Roosevelt Administration, exercised in part through his own writings, and in part through Felix Frankfurter, has been very much greater than is generally realized." Laski, he noted, argued in the book that liberalism "has always suffered from its inability to realize that great possessions mean power over men and women as well as over things." Laski's error, he suggested, was in overlooking the fact "that this grave moral defect is to be remedied merely by increasing the scope and authority of the State is a perfect *non sequitur*. It is curious that Mr. Laski should see so clearly in fascism those dangers of totalitarianism which he completely ignores in the communist state."[2]

In early August, Morley attacked an Ickes campaign speech with an editorial captioned "Mr. Ickes on Progressivism," writing that Ickes had revealed one of the most critical weaknesses of the New Deal—its "contempt for 'practical' methods of attacking grave national problems," with the result that many of the New Deal programs had failed. Recovery could come about only by substituting "methods and policies tested by experience for happy-go-lucky pursuit of 'progressive' ideals."[3] A month later Morley returned to the theme with an editorial on an FDR speech, writing that FDR and the New Dealers had "their vision fixed so intently upon the more abundant life that they frequently ignore the first principles of good government and sound economics," and had failed "to adopt practical means of attaining Utopian objectives," in particular constitutional ones.[4]

Meanwhile, Landon's campaign had caused Morley to lose heart in the Republican alternative to Roosevelt. After a series of Landon speeches that ranged from "poor" to "bad," Morley wrote that it was now "a virtual impossibility for me to support Landon, who is proving more of a disappointment because he started out so well." Roosevelt, he wrote, had "done some appalling things, but he seems to me to have the capacity for growth and I am beginning to doubt that Landon does." How different from Morley's misgivings a few months earlier at the time of the Democratic Convention![5] Ten days later, however, Landon rallied with Morley as the result of his speech in Chicago on the budget.[6] By contrast, a Roosevelt speech in Chicago in mid-October revealed him to Morley as "a consummate rabble-rouser." Morley expected him to be reelected, and then, he confided to his journal, "will come the final test of his character: Will he move toward administrative improvement and effective consolidation of the social gains so far attempted? Or will he continue to seek to arrogate more powers to himself until all significant attributes of the federal form of government cease to exist?"[7]

In 1936, Hiram Johnson wrote of the forthcoming presidential campaign that it was "not going to be, in reality, political, but a class war."[8] When the campaign took the form he had predicted Johnson did not find it appealing. Remarkably, he even told his son that Hoover's speeches against the New Deal were the best being made. His enthusiasm for Roosevelt was fast waning, in part because he found the growing militancy of John L. Lewis and other non-AFL labor leaders, and Roosevelt's apparent endorsement of their radical methods, disquieting.[9]

Late in the campaign, he wrote to his son: "With ten million voters bought in this campaign by the different agencies of the government, it is absurd to think that Landon can be successful," and he wondered why Roosevelt was "exhibiting fright," since any man could who could travel across the country doling out millions from the federal checkbook, plus the millions from Hopkins's relief organization and from the AAA, should retire from politics. Johnson estimated that Roosevelt went into the election with "8 million votes bought," while the GOP had to buy them "one by one," and without taxpayers' money.[10] Nevertheless, Johnson voted for FDR in 1936, although he did not campaign actively for him as in 1932.

TNR responded to FDR's landslide victory by asking what the voters had voted for. It answered the following:

It is almost impossible to point to one concrete proposal by the President for future action. The platform promised merely not to undo what had been done, and to continue the good work. There were a few general words about balancing the budget at the earliest possible moment, about reforming the civil service, about staying out of war. But in a larger sense, if Mr. Roosevelt has any mandate from the electorate, it is a mandate to remain President and do what he wishes.

How would Roosevelt use his "blank check," when his sphere of action seemed larger now than in March 1933?[11]

After Roosevelt's reelection, Hiram Johnson predicted that FDR would now "give free rein to his imagination" with "nobody to stop him, and but a few to protest." He expected all sorts of experiments, "some of which will give us the cold shivers," because the president would "really feel that he has been given a mandate by the people to do as he pleases, and there will be enough people in Congress anxious to truckle to him, that will enable him to do just as he desires."[12]

Corcoran certainly did not lose interest in popularizing Coyle's ideas after the 1936 election was over. For 1937, Corcoran was primarily interested in a book by Coyle on taxation, designed to encourage Americans to shoulder the necessary burden of taxes to accomplish the goals of his other books. The publisher wrote to Corcoran that the Coyle galley proofs were being returned by readers with enthusiastic comments. He suggested a larger-than-usual printing, but said it could only be done if there were substantial advance orders or subsidy, and he suggested federal agencies as potential purchasers.[13] Corcoran thanked those who contributed, writing that the "ripples should go far."[14]

To help achieve this ripple effectt, Corcoran arranged for Coyle's book, *Why Pay Taxes?*, to be serialized in two newspapers that supported the New Deal. He suggested it to the publisher of the *New-*

ark Ledger, noting that it was already being serialized in the *New York Post* and the Philadelphia *Record.* Nothing could help the New Deal more, he told the publisher, than to reprint "this illuminating serial," which dealt with the serious problem of educating the American people to the need for higher taxes.[15] Proofs also went from Corcoran to Congressman Gerald Voorhees, of California, for serialization in a Los Angeles newspaper.[16]

The book that Corcoran was so avidly publicizing to help the New Deal was one Coyle had written to educate the American people for the higher taxes that he advocated. In *Why Pay Taxes?* Coyle wrote:

As modern life becomes more and more complicated, the need for planned adjustment grows more pressing. But the task of arranging all the multitudinous details into a rational system seems each year farther beyond the capacity of the human mind. Realistic people are coming to the belief that a well designed use of economic forces, such as taxation, is the way of escape from the over-complexity of economic problems. By such means it may be possible to reduce the area of detailed planning and detailed regulation to somewhere within the bound of human capacity.

The federal budget, Coyle wrote, was what economists called an "open-market operation." He explained:

That is, the Government buys more or less goods and services from the people, which has an effect on business, whether the effect is planned or accidental. We can get better results by recognizing this fact, and planning this operation to give us the effects we want. Whatever we do or don't do, the budget is going to have an influence, good or bad. We had better manage it so as to have a good influence. . . . [W]e may make up our minds to work for a heavy surplus in good times and a heavy deficit in hard times. If we do that, on a large enough scale, there is a chance to calm the capitalist system and stop it from hitting the ceiling and the floor and perhaps breaking its venerable bones.[17]

Here was a clear distinction between managing the economy and planning it.

After Roosevelt's reelection, Frankfurter suggested that Bliven publish in *TNR* an expose of the evils in the "behavior of the press," in particular,

a supplement exposing with vivid power what has been done in this campaign through headlines, suppressions, falsifications, etc. etc. etc., in what purported to be news or statements of fact. And I would take by way of examples The Chicago Tribune, The New York Herald Tribune, and the Hearst press. . . . You will thus be furnishing powerful ammunition throughout the country and helping to destroy—what seems to me so vital to destroy, or at least undermine—some of the evil symbols and some of the powerful sources for evil-doing in the future.[18]

A few weeks later he made a further suggestion, writing Bliven the following:

I know not what you think but, for me, the single greatest danger in going forward in the next few years is the creation of a fake "era of good feeling." Those who know what they're about sedulously engage in trying to affect the minds of those who, in an uncritical or soft-hearted way, don't know what those who are about are about. Winthrop Aldrich's speech yesterday is part of this effort, and he gives you an opportunity of doing what I think is so important to do, namely, to expose false symbols that so often exert powerful influence on American public opinion. Specifically, have someone go through Aldrich's speeches during the last four years—the noble things he said during the early days of the New Deal, the reactionary things he said particularly in the last stages of the campaign, and the song he is now singing immediately after the election.[19]

Thus did Frankfurter seek to advance the cause of class conflict and to emasculate press criticism by discrediting the most critical of the newspapers.

As FDR's second administration began in 1937, Bliven and *TNR* lowered their goals to be somewhat more realistic and in tune with the administration's objectives. The president's pledge to raise the standard of living of the "one third of a nation ill-housed, ill-clad, ill-nourished," caused the magazine, as Seideman said, to stand by Roosevelt "as never before."[20] One aspect of the new relationship with the New Deal was the launching of the offensive against its journalistic critics—both columnists like Walter Lippman, Frank Kent, and Dorothy Thompson, and newspapers like the *Chicago Tribune* and the *Los Angeles Times*, not to mention the Hearst chain—that Frankfurter had suggested.

When early in 1937 Roosevelt sent to Congress his proposal for reorganization of the federal courts in such a way as to add to the Supreme Court enough new judges to make a majority, collectivists were supportive. With a majority obedient to Roosevelt, the way would be open to resume the collectivist march of the first New Deal. *TNR* wrote a few days after FDR submitted his court-packing proposal:

However concealed may be the political motive [behind the Court's decisions], it is almost invariably there; the political consequences of its constitutional judgments are obvious to all. It is furthermore obvious that the general trend of these decisions is conservative; that taken all in all they prevent the other branches of government from acting to alleviate social and economic ills. So drastic and far-reaching have been a number of these recent decisions that most informed persons are hopeless that government will be able to cope with the tasks thrust upon it in the modern world so long as we have the same Supreme Court as now or so long as we have the same Constitution. A crisis of some sort is upon us. Something has to be done about the Court or the Constitution or both. This is essentially a political job, in the sense that it must spring from and emphasize the will of the people. These premises automatically cancel the objections to the President's proposal from the Right, from those who believe that the Supreme Court has been the embodiment of wisdom and has saved us from the perils of democratic institutions. . . . Objections from the Left grant that something must be done, but charge that this is not the right way to do it. It is an undignified subterfuge to "pack the Court." If a liberal can do it, a conservative could also. In view of the difficulty of predicting how Justices will decide, packing may be ineffective in any case. . . . It would be better to limit the powers of the Court by legislation or constitutional amendment, or to extend the powers of government by amendment.

TNR was not receptive to the opposing arguments of either the left or right, concluding the following:

Some effective way or ways must be found of registering a national desire that the Court act differently at the present time. "Packing" the Court is as good a way to do this as any. . . . The very fact that a series of reactionary decisions led to a strongly supported proposal to pack the Court will of itself, no matter what happens as a result of this bill, exert a potent influence on the Court in the future. The learned Justices are bound to be a little more careful not to clothe their private prejudices in the Constitution, or to veto in the name of that broad document measures that the nation has decided it needs.[21]

A week later Leon Green in *TNR* addressed the charges that "the proposal puts the Court under the power of the President and makes him a dictator." According to *TNR*, that was an "exaggeration" coined from "desperation," since any "new Judges will be as free as the present ones are," and the constitution was "adhered to both in form and spirit." Then, somewhat in contradiction of the foregoing, the author continued,

By the last election the people through their confidence in President Roosevelt and his measures directed him and the Congress to keep this way of government in operation. His proposal is in keeping with that vote. Political? Yes. Who supposes it could be otherwise? It is the only method available for exerting governmental control over the judiciary in the exercise of its functions, or keeping it working in harmony with other departments of government, and I suppose no one thinks the Supreme Court is not a part of our government and not subject to political control, however remote it may be.[22]

Unfortunately, *TNR* soon discovered that some of the most effective opposition to Roosevelt's plan was coming from those whom even it had to admit were liberals. Early in March it wrote,

The real danger to the bill comes ... from progressive Senators and Representatives who sincerely want something done about the Court and the Constitution, but do not want it done in this way. To them it appears that the necessary permanent reform is a constitutional amendment, and that the President's proposal is an inferior substitute that will let off the steam of protest which might otherwise be utilized as pressure behind what they believe is a more fundamental measure. This position is worthy of respect, and those who hold it are entitled to something better than massed opposition or ridicule. Though we believe they would damage the objectives in which they are interested if their action caused the defeat of the present bill, we can see that their attitude may be turned to good use. ... The progressives in Congress will be accepting a heavy responsibility indeed if they allow the present tactics of the reactionaries to build up such an obstruction against doing anything about the Court and the Constitution that the opportunity will be lost for many years to come. And that—make no mistake about it—is just what the reactionaries are hoping to do, with the practical but unwitting aid of these very progressives.[23]

In March 1937, *The New Republic* opened its pages to an article by Laski on "An Englishman Looks at the Court." Not surprisingly, Laski championed Roosevelt's attempt to pack the Supreme Court, writing that "the President's proposals need neither explanation nor defense." He explained:

Much recent American jurisprudence is literally unintelligible except upon the assumption that the Constitution intended the judges permanently to safeguard the rights of property as these were understood in the age of laissez-faire. The Supreme Court has, by a majority, chosen to adopt a political philosophy whose major premise is the protection of capitalism from any serious control by the federal government. It is not surprising that even so moderate a liberal as President Roosevelt should, after the experience of the last four years, conclude that such a conception of the judicial office is wholly at variance with the needs of the modern state.

Since 1932 it has been difficult to distinguish the philosophy of the Supreme Court from that of Wall Street. It was not to maintain that identity that President Roosevelt was returned triumphantly to the the White House.

That a Marxist should object to a Supreme Court that had voided the New Deal's experiments in collectivism ought not to be surprising. But in seeking to identify himself with liberals, Laski concluded: "Liberals all over the world should rejoice that so early in his second term he has set out to deal forthrightly with the central problems of American administration."[24]

A month later FDR wrote to his secretary Miss Le Hand, "I want to see Laski. Get hold of him somehow. Either Tues. April 13th or Tues. April 20th. Best thing to do is to have him for luncheon."[25] In May, Frankfurter wrote Laski: "Here not much has happened since you left except that during F.D.R.'s absence his enemies have been talking big. Also there is a growing endeavor to have Ben [Cohen] and Tom [Corcoran] take the place of Tugwell as the big bogie. But I think it will be difficult to build up that kind of a new scare."[26] A week later, after a visit with FDR, Laski wrote to Miss Le Hand that it had been "grand to see him in such fighting form. I hope he was not disappointed by the report of the Senate Judiciary Committee [which killed Roosevelt's court proposal]. That kind of blindness is, I think, the necessary prelude to light."[27] Later Laski wrote Frankfurter:

I can't say I was surprised at F.D.'s defeat over the Court. It looks as though there must be a deeper appreciation of the nature of the forces in battle before the significance of the Court as the true veto-power is understood. I hope he makes the right appointment [to the court] in [the retiring Justice] Van Devanter's place; and at this distance, the urgent thing looks like the need on his part for a big offensive this autumn on social legislation really to bring the judges up against it. If they accept it, well and good; if not, the battle can be reopened on a larger terrain.[28]

Hereafter Laski and Frankfurter would encourage Roosevelt in confrontation with the court.

By its essays on the court issue, *TNR* showed the extent to which it was out of touch with the sentiment of the nation at large, as well as that of many liberals. It was also out of touch with the mood in Congress, predicting that Roosevelt's plan would be approved by that body in some form within "the next ten days."[29] Seideman writes, "The editors' spirited defense of Roosevelt marked a radical turning point for the magazine and the start of a new realism."[30] Suddenly *TNR* began to sing praises of the New Deal's accomplishments, including even the oft-criticized WPA.

When the president sent his court proposal to Congress, Lippmann headlined his column "The Seizure of the Court." It was a proposal, he wrote, whose "audacity is without parallel in American history, [for] no President has ever dreamed of asking for the personal power to remake the court to suit himself, [one that would] interpret the Constitution as he wished to have it interpreted. If the American people do not rise and defeat this measure, then they have lost their instinct for liberty and their understanding of constitutional government." He added, "I do not say that Mr.Roosevelt is a dictator or that he wishes to be one. But I do say that he is proposing to create the necessary precedent, and to establish the political framework for, and to destroy the safeguards against, a dictator. As he would revolutionize the practice of government, a dictator would need to obtain only one transient and hysterical majority. Once in power, he would be free to remodel the Constitution to suit himself." It was the greatest issue raised in America since secession, he wrote. The question was whether "the people shall be deprived of their sovereign right to give and to withhold the powérs their servants exercise, or whether a man, who has evaded the judgment of the people on this very question, shall by indirection become the master of all three branches of the government and of the fundamental law as well." If successful, it would amount to a Rooseveltian "coup d'etat."[31]

Later that month Lippmann wrote a thoughtful analysis of what he called "the deep difference between normal progressivism and Mr. Roosevelt's emergency progressivism." Except for the N.R.A., he observed, liberals and progressives had supported virtually every aspect of the New Deal, differing only over "ways and means, about the size of the expenditures, about the quality of the administrative acts, about the temper and spirit when it has been reckless and terroristic." Now, however, he found that most liberals had ceased to support the president because he had "gradually ceased to think of himself as a servant of the democracy and has begun to think of himself as a man designated to impose and provide the desirable reforms." Roosevelt appeared to believe, as all "undemocratic leaders," believed, "that the people will follow them, and that the rules of democracy have been suspended for their benefit." "True" progressives did not adhere to such beliefs, and recognized in Roosevelt's court scheme "the unmistakable marks of that personal government which is wholly incompatible with democracy."[32]

Late in April, Lippmann delivered a lecture at Johns Hopkins University on "The Rise of Personal Government in the United States." To his audience, Lippmann listed the transfers of power, actual and requested, to Roosevelt's hands since his inauguration. The president, he pointed out, had

asked Congress to delegate to him the legislative power over economic affairs, the legislative power of appropriation over half the budget, the legislative power to define the statutory functions of the Executive branch of the government, the administrative control of the independent quasi-judicial commissions, and he has asked the Supreme Court to consent to his control over the personnel and over the opinions of the independent commissions.

Roosevelt had also created "the most powerful political machine that has ever existed in the history of this country," by use of which he exercised "the power of life and death over governors, mayors, county officials, Senators and Representatives," and also controlled "by means of direct subsidies or favors of one kind and another large compact organized minorities in almost every constituency." He had used the powers delegated to him by Congress to pack Congress with men who were his puppets, and he had now asked Congress for authority to do the same thing to the Supreme Court. The supreme irony of it all was that this march toward dictatorship was being led by people who called themselves liberals! Lippman pointed out, "It is a grim joke that people who call themselves liberals should be so busy undermining their own—and other people's—liberty, while all the time they think they are buttressing it."[33]

With Roosevelt reelected overwhelmingly for another four years, *The Nation*, like *TNR*, had begun to write more positively of him. Stuart Chase wrote of the president, "Short of revolution, he has brought about reforms and breaches of the old order so colossal as to stagger the imagination."[34] However, a major obstacle had emerged even to what The Nation regarded as Roosevelt's limited efforts—the Supreme Court. The editors agreed with Max Lerner's assessment that the court was "smashing the best legislative efforts of the community," by which they meant primarily collectivist efforts.[35] In numerous editorials *The Nation* criticized the Court for reenforcing states' rights at the expense of the centralized powers that had been granted by Congress to the executive branch under the New Deal. Kirchwey's biographer writes that *"The Nation* seemed to come to life about the issue of curbing the power of the Supreme Court."[36]

The Nation began with forthright support for Roosevelt in his effort to pack the Supreme Court, writing in mid-February 1937, that the confrontation between Roosevelt and the Supreme Court was the greatest since the Dred Scott case. The Supreme Court, having shown so little respect for the welfare of workers and farmers that they had nullified New Deal legislation, deserved the opprobrium of the people and their elected representatives. *The Nation* was confident that the president would win.[37] A few days later it added that "Roosevelt's attack on government by senility has been a brilliant tour de force," leaving the nation both "puzzled and entertained." It questioned whether Roosevelt's proposal was the best way to attack the problem, but argued that it was the duty of liberals to support the bill, "with an open-eyed awareness of its shortcomings," since it would eliminate the Supreme Court as an obstacle to the New Deal.[38] But, *The Nation* added that it should be accompanied by an amendment to curb the powers of the court.[39]

A week later a writer in *The Nation* was still confident that "Roosevelt Will Win." Paul Ward, the journal's Washington correspondent, wrote that despite the furor surrounding Roosevelt's court-packing plan, "when all the shouting and the tumult dies, the nation will find that Roosevelt has at last achieved his objective." But liberals and radicals should not allow their support of the proposal to distract them from the larger goal of an amendment to the Constitution to protect the people from the "prejudices" of any future court. Liberals and radicals should also seize the opportunity to barter their support for legislative commitments from the Roosevelt administration that would include additional attacks on business.[40]

Late in that momentous month, Max Lerner took up the opposition of Walter Lippman to the court-packing plan.

For two weeks I have followed anxiously the serialized account of Walter Lippmann's hopes and fears for the Constitution. I had two reasons for my religious pursuit. Here, I felt, in these flowers plucked from Mr. Lippmann's corner of the *Herald Tribune* crannied wall, I should get at the secret of his whole universe. And here too I should find summed up the mature thinking of conservatives on the constitutional issue.

In the first I was not disappointed. I found everything in Mr. Lippmann's career rolled up in these six articles as in a single ball. Something in his subject had clicked with him as never before. I found spread out before me the entire anatomy of his mind—his easy expository tone, his dialectical skill, his genius for clarity to the point of barreness, his rhetoric, which is always just on the point of becoming eloquence, his magisterial air, his talent for opening his mind to no more of his subject than for the moment he cares to admit, his tone of fairness, his capacity for concealing the impulsions of his thinking while laying bare its framework, the smugness about his own motives and the attribution of dishonesty to others which I can only describe as a moral megalomania. And I found in addition what one finds when the usually cold Mr. Lippmann gets really excited—a sort of glacial hysteria that fascinated me by its union of opposites.

The second part of my quest was disheartening. Clearly Mr. Lippmann is heir to the whole tradition of American political thought. What use does he make of it? Confronted by President Roosevelt's plan for reorganizing the Supreme Court he calls it dastardly, dishonest, reactionary, "audacious, ingenious and at bottom stupid"—an act of "usurpation," a "bloodless coup d'etat" which strikes at the "moral foundations of the republic."

Lippmann, he wrote, "does not want to achieve real legislative flexibility. He thoroughly distrusts Congress, as he distrusts every organ of the people. He wants to intrench minority rule. . . . And it is a tribute to Mr. Lippmann's intellectual athleticism that he can glorify minority rule in the name of democracy."[41]

Kirchwey took on those critics of the plan who viewed it as a step in the direction of dictatorship by insisting that there was not, in Roosevelt's proposal, even "the slightest sign of such a dictatorship in Mr. Roosevelt's plan," but that it was, on the contrary, a necessary step "in blocking the road to fascism." It was the court, she wrote, that had contributed to the "economic chaos out of which fascism grows" by its "refusal to allow national action for economic control." *The Nation* urged fellow "progressives" to ignore the "myth of Supreme Court divinity."[42]

But after a month of this, Oswald Garrison Villard, former owner and editor of the journal, and still an influential "editorial associate," challenged *The Nation*'s support for Roosevelt's plan from the point of view of traditional liberalism that was close to Lippmann's position. In an essay titled, "What is *The Nation* Coming To?" Villard took up the attacks by the magazine's columnist Heywood Broun on opponents of the court plan and wrote that those attacks were so vicious Villard "would conceal, if I could, my opposition to the Roosevelt method of achieving the Supreme Court reform I have urged so long." He continued:

Unfortunately [while in the West Indies] . . . I wrote a piece for some newspapers telling where I stood, in utter unawareness that I was thereby reading myself out of lifelong liberal associations. So now I am a recreant liberal gone tory, a miserable person who would fiddle with a constitutional amendment while America burns—with shame for Nine Old Men. . . . What has covered me with humiliation most of all are these words of Broun's: "On which side are you going to fight? Are you going to fight standing beside Bishop Manning, A. Lawrence Lowell, the *Herald Tribune*, the Liberty League, and William Randolph Hearst? Make up your mind."

Nothing else has revealed so clearly my present baseness, the falsity of my standards and values. How much time have I not wasted during these long years trying to assay rights and wrongs, seeking to get facts, endeavoring to weigh ethical values and to balance the merits and demerits of every proposal! How much, much easier it would have been always to have asked: "Where stand Manning and Hearst, James H. Rand, A. Lawrence Lowell, Henry Cabot Lodge, President Harding, the war-makers, the patrioteers, and all the others I have hated or despised?" And then to have stood against them. But after all, it is not quite so easy, for there are times when even a tory blunders on to the right side.

That I live in another day and age was clear to me when I read recently in The Nation—the same journal which fought so hard against Grant's proposal to pack the court—an appeal by Professor Karl N. Llewellyn of Columbia Law School, calling on us to join "the anti-tory front," although he admits that the President's proposal "is unfortunate from every angle but one." So, as Dorothy Thompson says, let us joyously go forward with such advanced and radical thinkers and curbers of the court as Jim Farley, Joe Robinson, Homer Cummings, and Pat Harrison—bedfellows whom Heywood Broun has loved so dearly in the past.[43]

An opening having been provided by Villard's article, there followed two weeks later a letter representing the views of the financial backers of the magazine. Maurice Wertheim wrote,

Those who control the Foundation which owns The Nation believe in the principle of editorial freedom. To insure it further they have, as you know, turned over to you, for a period, complete control of the paper in legal form. Because of my association with the Foundation and the fact that those who control it have no part in shaping The Nation's policies I feel that I must record my own personal dissent from your editorial policy on the President's Supreme Court program.

I do this in a spirit similar to that evidenced by my esteemed associate, Mr. Oswald Garrison Villard, in his recent article . . . wherein he discussed the same subject. I agree with him that the policy of the paper on this issue has been a mistaken one. Since The Nation was one of the first advocates, even before the President raised the issue, of a constitutional amendment to curb usurpation of power by the Supreme Court it has, I believe, lost a great opportunity in not realizing that advocacy of the President's proposal betrays its own cause.

Adding new members to the court actually sets the stamp of government approval upon a continuation of the legislative function by interpretation—only in the opposite direction. That is as plain as a pikestaff.

I am forced to the conclusion that this represented an unreflective stand. That the Constitution should be amended in order to narrow the interpretative power of the court on laws passed by the people's representatives is now being generally accepted. That we need more progressive legislation is likewise generally conceded. But why should The Nation—which has so resolutely opposed everything which even smacked of the authoritarian idea—allow itself to be caught by the bait of a few immediate laws which, as its own Washington correspondent, Mr. Paul Ward, pointed out in a recent issue, may not prove to be so progressive after all? Should not The Nation explore more deliberately the dangers inherent in this situation and call to the attention of its readers all its implications?

It amounts to this—that for the promise of immediate progressive legislation we are asked to sacrifice the great democratic principle that fundamental changes in our system of government shall result only from the decision of the people. Is it not clear beyond question, and does The Nation not know that it is clear beyond question, that the people have not passed on this subject and have not given the present Administration, as has been claimed, a mandate to do what the President now proposes. . . . It is a clear, bald attempt to grasp power—a thing not in the least to be condoned because it may be, and I believe it was, well intentioned—that is, with the purpose of securing progressive legislation sooner than would be possible via the democratic route.

The people of this country want their courts to be respected. It is unthinkable that a progressive and liberal journal should actually advocate any plan by which new judges are placed on our supreme tribunal who will decide cases on instructions, or who will be believed to have decided them on this basis.

Finally, does The Nation approve of the camouflage arguments concerning aging judges and congested dockets under cover of which it was attempted to slip this proposal through? Does it approve of all the mass of innuendo attributing dust storms, floods, and various other acts of God to the Supreme Court? I cannot believe it possible. The Nation has lost itself in judicial partisanship at a moment when I, for one, should like to see it come out, like Senator [Burton K.] Wheeler, Oswald Garrison Villard, and many other liberals, and say to the President: "Enough of his camouflage; enough of these attempts to discredit your adversaries as 'defeatist lawyers'; we like your objectives, but we don't like your methods. You can now attain your objectives with no sacrifice of American principles if you will not be stubborn. And if that be treason, make the most of it."[44]

The spankings administered by Villard and Wertheim led Broun to question in mid-April, "Is There a Nation?" in a column by that title. Broun wrote:

I do not know whether I will come again to this pasture. I'm getting a little sick of The Nation's policy of fair play, and everybody must be heard whether or not he has anything to say. This isn't an amateur tennis match. It's a fight, and the well-being of masses of men and women, depends upon the result. So I am not for the principle of bowing to your adversary and remarking, "After you, sir." Even an open mind needs to pull down the windows at certain times or it becomes less a mind than a cave of the winds. And speaking of open minds, before I put up the shutters I am curious to know just who it is who owns The Nation. All I can say is that the pottage isn't very hot and the service is something terrible.[45]

The issue was clear: Who was to exert editorial control of *The Nation*—its editors or its owners? Wertheim decided to sell *The Nation* and offered it first to Kirchwey. The alternative was to offer it on the open market to the highest bidder, a move which might only exacerbate the problem. Kirchwey raised the money and bought the journal.

Editorial and financial control were now centered in *The Nation*'s editor and the journal's "militant liberalism" could now go forward.[46] She remained convinced that fascism was "the natural outgrowth of capitalist-democracy at a certain point in its decadence."[47] Heywood Broun, perhaps disenchanted by *The Nation*'s position over the Supreme Court packing issue, approached *TNR* and told Bliven "he now likes The New Republic very much more than The Nation. He feels that we know where we are going, do a better job, and hew to the line, whereas The Nation he feels is inclined to vacillate. He said he would work for whatever price we were willing to pay . . . and so we made the arrangement."[48]

For her part, Kirchwey felt impelled to try to smooth over the differences between two of her columnists and end an editorial war before it had gone too far. It could only furnish comfort to the enemy, she wrote. "If liberals and progressives are going to be at each other's throats all the time it will make it very easy for the enemy to walk off with the victory."[49] According to Kirchwey's biographer she "considered a schism among the left to be very dangerous." While aware of the dangers and faults of the communists, she nevertheless considered even them capable of performing "necessary functions in the confused struggle of our time" as allies in the "antifascist struggle." This required that commonalties rather than differences be emphasized by opponents of the right wing groups.[50]

David Cushman Coyle was less concerned about the court-packing proposal than the motives behind it, since he saw clearly that it would give a second wind to the collectivism of the first New Deal. It had no relevance to the new direction FDR was now pursuing, one more in line with Brandeisian goals and tactics. It was not the Brandeis–Coyle New Deal that was encountering difficulties with the Court, nor was there any real prospect that it would. But in 1937 Roosevelt had begun to push a program that bore resemblances to the early New Deal in, for example, his desire for the government to take control of the wages and hours of industry through a board or commission. Coyle wrote Corcoran of his worry that Roosevelt was focusing on wages and hours legislation as the main issue in the court fight, which could only lead again to the failures of the NRA days, when only the Civil Works Administration (CWA) had rescued the nation from disaster.[51]

— 7 —

Progressives and the Court

Roosevelt's proposal to pack the Supreme Court drove more liberals into opposition to the New Deal, as it seemed to confirm for them what critics like Pinchot had been charging all along—that the president and those around him were intent on creating a dictatorship. Norman Hapgood wrote Burt Wheeler that he thought it important to "get hold of Sinclair Lewis, possibly through his wife, [columnist] Dorothy Thompson, as she is working hard on the court matter. If Lewis would talk about his book "It Can't Happen Here," it would be a spectacular feature of the committee hearing." That book, of course, had been about the possible triumph of fascism in the United States. Hapgood also suggested that Wheeler put his hands on George Seldes's book, *Sawdust Caesar*, as an example "of how fast ideas change as soon as one person feels that he can do whatever he likes."[1] Similarly, Max Ascoli, whose skepticism concerning the "neo-liberals" of the 1930s had been growing, opposed the court-packing plan in an article for the *New York Herald-Tribune*.[2]

Pinchot addressed an open letter to all members of Congress on 13 February 1937, in which he charged that Roosevelt's proposal was meant "to empower Mr. Roosevelt to shape the findings of the Court so that, for the next four years at least, he will control the political and economic life of the country." Congress was regarded as little more than the "mouthpiece" of the president, as a result of "the threat of withheld patronage, the lash of propaganda and reprisals in home districts," which had left few of them independent. Now the nation faced a "situation in which both the legislative and judicial branches of the government will have ceased to function as anything but instruments of the White House." Passage of the court-packing bill would represent "a long and perhaps irrevocable step into dictatorship."[3]

Pinchot was appalled to find the Scripps–Howard newspapers still supporting the president, and he wrote his friend Roy Howard that he hated "to see your newspapers making a genuflection and giving a little high church episcopalian bob every time His name is mentioned . . . the time has come when he ought to be soundly spanked with a shingle with a nail in it every time he moves toward autocracy or springs economic doctrines which tend to keep the bread lines long." If Roosevelt's power weren't "clipped," he would no only "destroy himself but the Democratic party and raise hell with the country at a time when it is just getting on its feet."[4] It was "embarrassing for liberals to have to fight on the same side with economic royalists," he wrote. "But even economic royalists have moments when their efforts are for the public good, as well as their own."[5] To Rabbi Stephen Wise he wrote, "No matter how liberal a man may be there comes a time when he must measure alleged liberalism by the standard of common sense."[6]

Late in April Pinchot addressed a public letter to the president, in which he wrote of an issue that had been raised by Federal District Judge John Knox in testimony before the Judiciary Committee relating to Section 2 (a) of the court bill:

As Judge Knox points out, this section means that the government may arrange things so that only the new district and circuit court judges, whom you will appoint, will be transferred to other districts in order to try cases in which the government may be especially interested.

Judge Knox, a most able and experienced jurist, who, by the way, has been a life-long Democrat and a good friend of your administration, says that this section "exhibits a consistency of purpose that is of sinister aspect to every man who, on principle, is opposed to the use of stacked decks of cards." The sort of power that this bill would put in your hands is so alien to the American tradition of an impartial judiciary that it is hard for me to imagine that you either know or approve its purpose.

The sinister purposes of the bill transmitted from the White House having been brought to light, Pinchot wrote, "We are loath to attribute these purposes to you. But who were the men who drafted the bill? And why have their names been kept secret? . . . Why should the names of men who have drawn a bill which, if passed, will turn this country back toward autocracy be so carefully hidden from Congress and the people?"

Pinchot then addressed Roosevelt's failure to produce recovery from the depression, the root cause of which he found in the New Deal's failure to increase industrial production. He wrote, "In fact, production seems to be the one thing in which it is supremely uninterested, it's emphasis always being on redistribution." But mere redistribution of wealth could "not considerably help the wage-earner, or the consumer—who seems as usual to be starring in the role of Forgotten Man—unless production expands," providing more wealth to distribute. But production could "not thrive on uncertainty, or on fear, or in handcuffs. And such as existed under the New Deal, with the result that the "United States has had a slower rate of recovery than any democratic nation in the world. Our index of production is below the average of the world. And our relief rolls are proportionally the largest in the world. We have half of the total reported unemployment in the world." Unfortunately, in the New Deal "mecca of advanced thinking, the opinion of social workers and Greenwich Village philosophers, who have little understanding of production and distribution, is accepted as the last word of wisdom." The sooner these "professional breast-heavers and friends of the masses" were sent back "to their settlement houses and classrooms . . . the better it will be for the country, especially including labor," because the United States was still a capitalist and industrial nation based on the profit system, and "till this is changed, and we cross the magic line into socialism or fascism, or whatever it may be, the notion that there is something sinful and outrageous about making a profit is sheer nonsense." Returning to the judiciary bill, Pinchot observed that many opponents of the bill were denying that they believed FDR aspired to be a dictator. But Pinchot wrote that he could not agree with their reasoning. Having watched Roosevelt's "steady and unrelenting drive for more and more power," he had been "forced to conclude that, whatever your undisclosed purpose may be, you desire the power of a dictator without the liability of the name."[7]

A month later Pinchot received a copy of a letter historian James Truslow Adams had sent to the National Commitee to Uphold Constitutional Government, an organization publisher Frank Gannett and others had formed to oppose Roosevelt over the judiciary bill. In the letter Adams reported having lunched with a "very important American, who has known the President since boyhood." When

Adams asked him whether he thought FDR harbored any idea of being a dictator, the answer was: "I do not think that he regards himself at all as a dictator in the European sense, but since his recovery from paralysis he has become utterly fearless and would break any precedent. He also has come to consider that he alone can be the saviour of the United States and knows what is best for it." Adams considered this "a dangerous situation." And, having read over Roosevelt's proposal for reorganizing the executive agencies, Adams found it "almost, if not quite, as dangerous as his reaching out for control of the Supreme Court. If he is not brought to a stop on some of these measures soon, we have got a dictator, which I could not have believed possible two or three years ago." Adams also reported that after he had attacked the president a year earlier, his income taxes had been completely audited by the Treasury Department, for the first time in eight years.[8] Democratic Senator Burton K. Wheeler, a leading opponent of the judiciary bill, likewise reported that "for the first time in my life, they have checked up on my income tax, and I wrote a letter to [Secretary of the Treasury] Henry Morgenthau telling him if he was attempting to stir up anything against me as was done in connection with Huey Long and some of his friends, that he was picking on the wrong man."[9] This was only further proof for Wheeler of the dangers inherent in the concentration of power the plan would create. Senator Wheeler recalled his own experiences in the Nonpartisan League in World War I, and was certain that without the Constitution and Bill of Rights backed up by the Supreme Court, he and his fellow liberals would all have been jailed. "It is an easy step," he learned, "from the control of a subservient Congress and the control of the Supreme Court to a modern democracy of a Hitler or a Mussolini."[10]

Within weeks after the second inauguration, Hiram Johnson's worst accumulating fears about Roosevelt had been validated, and the Californian was in full opposition. He wrote to his son early in February 1937 that he was opposing the Neutrality Bill, as another "sinister grab for power" by the president—the "war-making power." And if FDR succeeded in packing the Supreme Court, he would "make himself an absolute dictator in fact." He feared "that the next few years, with an unbalanced budget, with the expenditure of funds running wild, and a neutrality bill giving the President the war-making power, in reality, and with a Supreme Court subservient to him, we'll be very close to a Dictatorship." Congress, he conceded was "worse than subservient, and no one man can prevent what is happening."[11] A week later he added that Roosevelt's court plan marked "the breaking-down of the system we have become familiar with in this country. Down that road lies Dictatorship."[12]

Johnson was equally concerned about the lawlessness of the CIO's sit-down strikes, writing that "there is grave danger of running into a dictatorship in our Republic. If you will read Mussolini's 'March on Rome,' his ultimatum to the authorities, how all the industries of Italy were then in possession of workers, and how when the Government could do nothing, he cleaned up the whole situation, and the middle class rose to him, you will see how easy is the road to dictatorship."[13] His own attack on the CIO's actions had led, he told his son, "the little lick-spittles of the press" to accuse him "of being a 'Liberal' who had become a very bitter 'Tory,' and this despite the fact that [AFL head] William Green himself denounces this new warfare."[14]

As for Roosevelt's grasp for the Supreme Court, Johnson had long complained of the ability of "nine old men" to thwart the executive and legislative branches of the government through their antiquated interpretations of the Constitution, and had favored some sort of remedy. But given his accumulating doubts about Roosevelt, Johnson now viewed the president's action as more dangerous than the obstacles posed by the court. What concerned Johnson, as his biographer points out, was "the uses to which Roosevelt would put the legislation. With huge party majorities in both houses of Congress and a subservient court, he would effectively exercise dictatorial control." And that would be the likely result of his success, even if it were not his present object.[15]

But Johnson did not see how the president could be beaten. Through the use of patronage and the vast sums at his disposal, Roosevelt could doubtless control enough votes in Congress.[16] Weeks later, he wrote: "We can not deny he already has the legislative branch, and he whips it about as a schoolmaster would whip a recalcitrant boy. Give him now the judicial branch and all the power of government would be his. This way dictatorship."[17]

Then followed the Reorganization Bill, which Johnson, like many others, viewed as just another Rooseveltian grasp for power. It would, he wrote, give the president power "to do practically as he pleases with the various departments of government, and removes all checks." If the Court and Reorganization Bills were passed, Johnson did "not believe any man living could resist the power that will then be accorded him. This is on the theory that he is not seeking dictatorship, but I think the theory is not justified by the facts."[18] Referring to Roosevelt's "Dictator complex," Johnson wrote his son again: "Taken all in all, we are marching along that road that I have referred to before, but which few people recognize and few people care about. Roosevelt has won practically all his objectives."[19]

On 5 February 1937, Felix Morley penned his own reaction to the court proposal, writing that it was "the most dramatic and the most revolutionary step Roosevelt has yet taken." But Morley was convinced that "F.D.R. has out-smarted himself, as the saying goes. This essentially surreptitious and deceitful scheme will, as it is understood, arouse a wave of antagonism. Indeed it is very likely to cause the fundamental split in the Democratic Party which soon or late is foreordained. Roosevelt is getting into deep water, and . . . the clouds are rolling up."[20]

A month later Morley still believed Roosevelt had "overstepped the mark, especially as the industrial picture is brightening so markedly with promise of real collective bargaining." He did not expect labor to support Roosevelt's court proposal, nor the farmers, and business and the professions were "predominantly opposed."[21] He found Roosevelt's speech at the "Victory Dinner" in early March to be "a frontal attack on the Court, and therefore inferentially on the entire Federal system of government. No other interpretation is possible, though this time his presentation was rather less bitter than the text led me to expect." He continued that Roosevelt was suffering from an "easy confusion of Righteousness and Right," and seemed bent on bending "the traditional forms of American government out of recognition."[22] In a *Post* editorial, Morley bemoaned the fact that reason and a rational approach seemed at a disadvantage, while emotionalism and demagoguery were in the ascent.[23]

When Roosevelt, in a March "fireside chat" raised the bogey of a recurrence of 1929 conditions if his court-packing scheme were not approved, Morley wondered how "the 'nine old men' can be held responsble for the inflationary tendencies, or how 'young blood' on the bench could possibly hold these in check should they once get well-started." He found the Roosevelt administration using "a curious combination of deception, demagoguery and wheedling" in behalf of the court-packing bill," which indicated that the opposition was stronger than Roosevelt had expected. Morley conceded Roosevelt had a valid point in insisting that the powers of the federal government needed to be enlarged, but like many other liberals he insisted that the only proper device was through amendments to the constitution.[24]

After a March speech by Roosevelt in which the president had simultaneously boasted of recovery and warned of an impending crisis, Morley wondered how it was possible for Roosevelt to "both have his cake and eat it." It seemed clear to Morley an admission that either the New Deal had failed to solve the problems it confronted in 1933, or that it now faced new problems of its own creation. Roosevelt's attack, Morley pointed out, had ceased to be merely against the "nonconformist" members of the Supreme Court, but "against the Court as an institution, and thereby inferentially against the constitutional system which gives an independent judiciary the right to review legislation."[25]

By late March 1937, Morley had begun to address "the inflationary tendencies regarding which [FRB Chairman Marriner] Eccles and other Administration leaders are beginning to voice open concern." Secretary of Agriculture Henry A. Wallace was insisting that the federal government needed "more power" to deal with the situation, when, in Morley's view they were in part the result of the New Deal's already "enormous powers" that it had "exercised in conflicting directions." It was a case of "some of Mr. Roosevelt's less attractive chickens . . . beginning to come home to roost."[26]

When Senator O'Mahoney, "a staunch Administration supporter who has turned against the Court plan," went on the offensive against it in May, Morley concluded that "the President's ill-judged attempt to tamper with the judiciary is now beaten. If so he has suffered the first substantial set-back—and probably a very healthy one for him—since he took office."[27]

In May 1937, Bruce Bliven sent to the President advance proof of an article that was to appear in the next issue of *TNR*. In it he had assembled conservative criticism of liberal reforms proposed during the past thirty years, "most of which have since been carried out and are now accepted by everyone." The point was to attempt to show that conservative opposition to the court-packing plan was simply another case of unwarranted conservative hysteria over the pospect of change.[28] Roosevelt responded that he was "delighted" to receive the advance proofs and that the "chronology is a striking one and shows impressively that much of the opposition to the proposed reorganization of the Federal Judiciary had its counterpart in past years when other reforms were under consideration."[29] Neither man had apparently yet grasped the reality of the overwhelming liberal–progressive opposition to the scheme.

The Supreme Court issue shattered Roosevelt's control over congressional Democrats. As Ekirch has observed, the president would never again be able to rally the large democratic majorities in Congress behind his "must" bills. Ekirch writes, "The bitter struggle not only alienated many of Roosevelt's followers, but it also split the ranks of the liberal intellectuals. There was now more than ever, as Max Lerner pointed out, confusion over the meaning of democracy and its association with New Deal reforms. And, for really the first interval since the depression, progressives as well as conservatives began to look again with real nostalgia to the older, traditional values of American life—values that seemed threatened at home as well as abroad."[30] Thomas Corcoran recalled that the Court issue "died slowly, only after crowding out a veritable garden of promising domestic programs, including comprehensive antitrust reform, government reorganization and extension of the [TVA] principle." Missing from Corcoran's list was the wages and hours bill that FDR was pushing in 1937, that was contra Brandeis.[31]

In July, with the court-packing plan defeated, Bliven lashed out at newspaper columnists, upon whom he laid much of the blame, in a *TNR* essay on "The Cassandra Racket." Bliven charged:

There are now in this country a group of daily-newspaper commentators on public affairs who have at least one thing in common. They unite in taking an extremely dark view of the future of America, and in writing about the danger of calamity so persistently and so completely to the exclusion of other topics that it is not unfair to say this is now their chief business. My reference is to Dorothy Thompson, Walter Lippmann, Mark Sullivan, David Lawrence, George Sokolsky, Frank Kent, and their admiring imitators. . . . All of them believe that this country is moving in a direction dangerous to historic American principles and to the peace and happiness of a majority of our citizens. Some of them profess a special knowledge and authority regarding the rise of fascism in Europe, and find repeated parallels between what happened a few years ago in Germany and Italy and what is happening here today. Several of them see a direct danger of a fascist or semi-fascist state in America because of the actions of President Roosevelt or John L. Lewis.

At the moment, their chief bitterness is of course against the proposal for reorganization of the Supreme Court.

The group of columnists whose chief members I have named have an influence in American life that many people probably do not realize. . . . While there are a few liberal columnists who are also widely syndicated, the conservative group that I have been discussing greatly outnumber them— I should guess, by at least ten to one. It would of course be easy to overestimate the influence of the conservatives. They and the papers in which their work appears were opposed to Mr. Roosevelt's reelection in 1936 by about two to one, and the readers of these papers voted the other way in almost precisely the same proportions. Nevertheless, these writers do wield a tremendous power, particularly between elections and at a time like the present, when the horizon, both at home and abroad, seems so dark and troubled.

Perhaps the most striking single fact about the members of this group is that all of them were once markedly progressive in their views, and made their reputations as spokesmen for the new order. . . . I do not doubt that most or all of these individuals still consider themselves progressives, despite the nearly unanimous opposite judgment of everyone else whose opinions should carry weight.

Bliven's conclusion was that, on the contrary, the Cassandra columnists were bent on maintaining the status quo, and that "it is impossible for thoughtful men to take them seriously."[32] Clearly, nothing in their opposition, or in that of others whose liberal–progressive credentials were as sound as were Bliven's, had caused him to reexamine his own claim to that label.

When Roosevelt appointed Senator Hugo Black to the Supreme Court, *TNR*'s response again contradicted its arguments in favor of the court-packing plan. Black's appointment, it wrote was "a shrewd political act." It explained, "Senator Black is as outspoken and faithful a supporter of the New Deal as could be found; it is unlikely that he would question the constitutionality of any measure that the President has advocated or will advocate. Thus the President increases the progressive majority on the Court, as he has wished from the beginning to do."[33]

More subtle, but nevertheless obvious, was *TNR*'s shift toward a new and stronger emphasis on Keynesian spending, with the result, Seideman has said, that *TNR* editorials began to resemble a textbook on the subject and "overflowed with short chapters on such theories as the 'multiplier principle.'"[34] "The editors' stress on the efficacy of pump priming and deficit financing, [he writes] reflected a heightened awareness of the inadequacy [perhaps 'futility' would have been a more appropriate word] of the brand of liberalism they heretofore had espoused. Idle discussions of planned and collectivized societies vanished from *TNR*'s pages."[35] It seemed a case of Laski losing out to Keynes, although one must recall Laski's prediction of the ultimate outcome of such a spending program.

One example of the confusion into which American liberalism had fallen in the 1930s is evidenced by Bliven's admonition to *TNR* editors that they not take sides in a dispute between pro and anti-Trotskyites. "It seems to me," he wrote them, "a mistake for us to weaken our influence by being definitely labeled on one side or the other in the quarrel among the American liberals." For Bliven, Trotskyites were liberals, but Lippmann and others whose liberal–progressive credentials predated his own were not![36]

Bliven had not, moreover, altered his views about capitalism. Smarting from attacks on *TNR* in *American Mercury* in 1938, Bliven wrote a spirited defense of himself and *TNR* in the *American Mercury*'s "The Other Side" section, in which he asserted that American society had "to be reorganized whether we like it or not." He continued:

We cannot go on with a system which, internally, produces one depression after another; and, externally, keeps the threat of war hanging over the world. It is obvious that we should never duplicate the conditions obtaining under either Communism or Fascism in European countries that have never had any experience with political democracy or with even our own limited degree of economic democracy. In every country, the solution is largely determined by the traditions, the habits of mind, the native characteristics of its people.

I am not much impressed by the frenzied howls of the Conservatives, which I find in *The American Mercury* and other places, regarding the "regimentation" of the New Deal. If these gentleman had gone and looked at regimentation in the totalitarian states in Europe, as I have, they would realize how nonsensical their complaints are. To say that Mr. Roosevelt is a Socialist or a Communist is the exact opposite of the truth. He is doing his best to make private Capitalism work well enough to endure.

I, also, am critical of the New Deal, but from a different point of view. I wish it had faced the problems more frankly than it has, and taken more effective steps to cope with them. I regret that there has not been more continuous policy in Washington, a steadier long-time view. I wish social–economic planning had really been tried, instead of only its first beginnings. I wish the New Deal had not listened so often to the voices of the Conservatives who don't understand economics and don't really know what is good for them or for the country. . . . I feel that our national welfare is too serious a matter for questions of broad, fundamental policy to be put into the hands of bungling, incompetent amateurs like the heads of our great corporations and our big banks.

We can't go back to the pre-machine age, even if we want to. We can't find another frontier unless we take over the moon. Planning of output in terms of markets has only started. Governmental interference will continue to grow, and I can think of nothing more futile than for the Conservatives to sit around making faces at it.[37]

A major event in the controversy within liberaldom in the 1930s was the publication of Walter Lippmann's book, generally abbreviated by the title *The Good Society*, in 1937. Written before the tempest over Roosevelt's court-packing plan, and before Lippmann's concerns over the president's grasp for personal power had reached full flower, the book nevertheless sounded the same alarms. All over the world, he wrote, the same phenomenon could be found in the efforts of governments to grapple with the problems of the 1930s. As Lippmann put it:

Their weapons are the coercive direction of the life and labor of mankind. Their doctrine is that disorder and misery can be overcome only by more and more compulsory organization. Their promise is that through the power of the state men can be made happy. Throughout the world, in the name of progress, men who call themselves communists, socialists, fascists, nationalists, progressives, and even liberals, are unanimous in holding that government with its instruments of coercion must, by commanding the people how they shall live, direct the course of civilization and fix the shape of things to come.

He wrote, "The premises of authoritarian collectivism, have become the working beliefs, the self-evident assumptions, the unquestioned axioms, not only of all the revolutionary regimes, but of nearly every effort which lays claims to being enlightened, humane, and progressive."[38]

It was as true of progressives, as it was of any others, Lippmann wrote, for

Nearly everywhere the mark of a progressive is that he relies at last upon the increased power of officials to improve the condition of men. Though the progressives prefer to move gradually and with consideration, by persuading majorities to consent, the only instrument of progress in which they have faith is the coercive agency of government. They can, it would seem, imagine no alternative, nor can they remember how much of what they cherish as progressive has come by emancipation from political dominion, by the limitation of power, by the release of personal energy from authority and collective coercion. For virtually all that now passes for progressivism in countries like England and the United States calls for the increasing ascendancy of the state; always the cry is for more officials with more power over more and more of the activities of men.[39]

Such liberals held that the traditional "liberal conception of the state belongs, as President Roosevelt once put it, to a 'horse and buggy' era." Lippmann wrote, "We belong to a generation that has lost its way . . . it has returned to the heresies of absolutism, authority, and the domination of men by men. Against these ideas the progressive spirit of the western world is one long, increasing protest."[40]

As for the new "liberals" in America, "They do not like dictatorships, the concentration camps, the censorship, the forced labor, the firing squads, or the executioners in their swallowtail coats. But in the modes of their thinking, the intellectuals who expound what now passes for 'liberalism,' 'progressivism,' or 'radicalism,' are almost all collectivists in their conception of the economy, authoritarians in their conception of the state, totalitarians in their conception of society." But contrary to what such liberals believed, a "collectivist society can exist only under an absolute state." Why? Sounding very much like Coyle, Lippmann wrote:

For in so far as men embrace the belief that the coercive power of the state shall plan, shape, and direct their economy, they commit themselves to the suppression of the contrariness arising from the diversity of human interests and purposes. They cannot escape it. If a society is to be planned, its population must conform to the plan; if it is to have an official purpose, there must be no private purposes that conflict with it. That this is the inexorable logic of the principle can be learned best by looking at what actual collectivists say and do when they are in power.

Although the "average collectivist" did not wish to go "all the way to the totalitarian state," there was "nothing in the collectivist principles which marks any stopping place short of the totalitarian state."[41] "And worse than this, the application of those principles is cumulative in effect. As long ago as 1844 Herbert Spencer pointed out that 'every additional state-interference strengthens the tacit assumption that it is the duty of the state to deal with all evils and secure all benefits' and at the same time there is a continually 'increasing need for administrative compulsion and restraints, which results from the unforeseen evils and shortcomings of preceding compulsions and restraints.'"[42]

As for planning, Lippmann wrote:

But who . . . is to decide what is to be the specific content of the abundant life? It cannot be the people deciding by referendum or through a majority of their elected representatives. For if the sovereign power to pick the plan is in the people, the power to amend it is there also at all times. Now a plan subject to change from month to month or even from year to year is not a plan; if the decision has been made to make ten million cars at $500 and one million suburban houses at $3000, the people cannot change their minds a year later, scrap the machinery to make the cars, abandon the houses when they are partly built, and decide to produce instead skyscraper apartment houses and underground railroads.

There is, in short, no way by which the objectives of a planned economy can be made to depend upon popular decision. They must be imposed by an oligarchy of some sort, and that oligarchy must, if the plan is to be carried through, be irresponsible in matters of policy. . . . The planning board or their superiors have to determine what the life and labor of the people shall be.

Not only is it impossible for the people to control the plan, but, what is more, the planners must control the people. They must be despots who tolerate no effective challenge to their authority. Therefore civilian planning is compelled to presuppose that somehow the despots who climb to power will be benevolent—that is to say, will know and desire the supreme good of their subjects. This is the implicit premise of all the books which recommend the establishment of a planned economy in a civilian society. They paint an entrancing vision of what a benevolent despotism could do. They ask—never very clearly, to be sure—that somehow the people should surrender the planning of their existence to "engineers," "experts," and "technologists," to leaders, saviors, heroes. This is the political premise of the whole collectivist philosophy. . . . It is the premise, too, of the whole philosophy of regulation by the state, currently regarded as progressivism. Though it is disguised by the illusion that a bureaucracy accountable to a majority of voters, and susceptible to the pressure of organized minorities, is not exercising compulsion, it is evident that the more varied and comprehensive the regulation becomes, the more the state becomes a despotic power as against the individual. For the fragment of control over the government which he exercises through his vote is in no effective sense proportionate to the authority exercised over him by the government.[43]

Having argued that collectivism must inevitably lead to totalitarianism, irrespective of the intentions of the collectivists, Lippmann now turned to contemporary progressives and found them "gradual collectivists" who hoped "by the gradualness of their methods to avoid the violence of dictatorship." Yet their hopes were doomed, he wrote, for "the gradual collectivist, under the banner of popular sovereignty, believes in the dictatorship of random aggregations of voters. In this theory the individual has no rights as against the majority, for constitutional checks and bills of rights exist only with the consent of the majority. Even the right of the majority to rule is at the mercy of any passing majority. For there is nothing in the doctrine of the sovereignty of the majority to preclude the abolition of majority rule by a vote of a majority."[44] Lippmann then returned to the incompatibility of planning with democracy:

It is evident that a regime of this sort is afflicted with an insoluble contradiction. In so far as it seeks to administer the economy under a rational and coherent plan, it must somehow prevent one majority from overriding the decision of a previous majority. For if a plan is to be carried out, it must be adopted and the people therefore conform. If they do not conform, if they are free at any time to agitate for amendments, the plan ceases to be a plan. It would not be a plan if its parts were not closely interrelated; if it is subject to continual change at vital points, the whole design has to be remade continually. Yet this must inevitably happen in a democracy, for the very essence of the democratic process is that the rulers are continually responsible to popular opinion, and unless that opinion is free to change, and in changing to alter the policy of the state, there is no democracy. The very essence of the conception of planning is that a design can be adopted to which the people will thereafter conform. That is equivalent to saying that a democratic people cannot have a planned economy, and that in so far as they desire a planned economy they must suspend responsible government.[45]

Yet despite what Lippmann saw as obvious contradictions between collectivist planning and democracy, he found it "difficult to exaggerate the practical influence on western society of these collectivists, who call themselves social democrats, Fabian socialists, evolutionary or revisionist socialists, or merely progressives," in persuading "the intellectual world that social improvement must come by magnifying the dominion by public officials." An example of such "gradual collectivism" he found "in the New Deal, as it existed before the Supreme Court of the United States invalidated it."[46]

By contrast, the first principle of liberalism . . . is that the market must be preserved and perfected as the prime regulator of the division of labor. . . . The liberal philosophy is based on the conviction that, except in emergencies and for military purposes, the division of labor cannot be regulated successfully by coercive authority . . . and that, therefore, the true line of progress is not to impair or to abolish the market, but to maintain and improve it.

Sounding like Adam Smith, Lippmann then wrote:

When the collectivist abolishes the market place, all he really does is to locate it in the brains of his planning board. Somehow or other these officials are supposed to know, by investigation and calculation, what everyone can do and how willing he is to do it and how well he is able to do it and, also, what everyone needs and how he will prefer to satisfy his needs. From the liberal point of view it is naive to suppose that any body of officials could perform that function in time of peace and in an economy of abundance for the whole wide world.[47]

Lippmann continued:

Thus, while liberalism must seek to change laws and greatly to modify property and contract as they are now recognized by the laws, the object of liberal reforms is to preserve and facilitate the division of labor in the existing exchange economy. . . . The liberal attack on monopoly, unfair competition, and necessitous bargaining has as its guiding purpose the maintenance of that equal opportunity which the exchange economy presupposes and a high degree of divided labor requires; the method by which liberalism controls the economy is to police the markets, to provide in the broadest sense honest weights and measures, to make the bargains represent the exchange of true equivalents rather than the victory of superior strength, inside information, legal privileges, conspiracies, secret combinations, corruption, and legalized sharp practices.[48]

Fundamentally, a liberal government was one of laws by contrast with the arbitrariness of rule by men. As Lippmann put it,

Constitutional restraints and bills of rights, the whole apparatus of responsible government and of an independent judiciary, the conception of due process of law in courts, in legislatures, and among executives, are but the rough approximations by which men have sought to exorcise the devil of arbitrariness in human relations. Among a people which does not try to obey this higher law, no constitution is worth the paper it is written on; though they have all the forms of liberty, they will not enjoy its substance. . . . The development of human rights is simply the expression of the higher law that men shall not deal arbitrarily with one another. . . . They stem from the right not to be dealt with arbitarily by anyone else, and the inescapable corollary of the rights of man is the duty of man not to deal arbitrarily with others.

The gradual encroachment of true law upon wilfulness and caprice is the progress of liberty in human affairs.[49]

Then, in words that might have described his conception of Roosevelt in 1937, Lippmann wrote:

To design a personal plan for a new society is a pleasant form of madness; it is in imagination to play at being God and Caesar to the human race. Any such plan must implicitly assume that the visionary or someone else might find the power, or might persuade the masses to give him the power, to shape society to the plan; *all such general plans of social reconstruction are merely the rationalization of the will to power.* For that reason they are the subjective beginnings of fanaticism and tyranny. To think in terms of a new scheme for a whole society is to use the idiom of authority, to approach affairs from the underlying premise that they can be shaped and directed by an overhead control, that social relations can be fabricated according to a master plan drawn up by a supreme architect.

The supreme architect, who begins as a visionary, becomes a fanatic and ends as a despot. For no one can be the supreme architect of society without employing a supreme despot to execute the design.[50] [Emphasis mine.]

— 8 —

The Good Society

It would not be amiss to regard Lippmann's *The Good Society* as an equivalent for the "New Deal Revolution" in America of Edmund Burke's *Reflections on the Revolution in France* a century and a half earlier. Just as the liberal Burke was aghast at the deviation from traditional liberalism embodied in the program of the radical "liberals" of the French Revolution, so was Lippmann disturbed by the implications of the popularity of collectivist "liberalism" in the 1930s. Moreover, *The Good Society* was a pointed repudiation of the points made by his earlier *TNR* colleague, Herbert Croly, in Croly's influential book *The Promise of American Life*, and of Laski's attempts to show the incompatibility of democracy and capitalism. In its rejection of collectivism *The Good Society* was closest to the views of Louis Brandeis and of the principal spokesman for his ideas in the 1930s, David Cushman Coyle.

To meet the assault from someone as distinguished as Lippmann, the two leading liberal journals trotted out dreadnoughts for their reviews of *The Good Society. The New Republic* featured Lewis Mumford in an undistinguished review titled "Mr. Lippmann's Heresy Hunt." Mumford derided Lippmann for having "chosen to validate the principles of human freedom by confusing them with the operations of a free market," and for branding "as fatuity and error, leading straight to dictatorship, almost every species of modern collectivism."[1]

The Nation turned to Max Lerner, whose review was headed "Lippmann Agonistes," and which began with the observation that the book marked Lippmann's "renunciation of the earlier Lippmann and his consolidation of the latter-day Lippmann. It marks also his renunciation of the latter-day liberalism and his plea for a return to the earlier liberalism of the Western world." Lerner went on to say that Lippmann was "fighting the new order and arguing for the Golden Age of the old order, but he is also and at the same time arguing against the premises of the younger Lippmann and making explicit a new set of premises for the older Lippmann."

Lippmann had attempted to dissect "collectivism" and to defend "liberalism," but had managed "to bungle both jobs woefully." Lerner explained:

In the first one he is never quite certain whether he is talking of dictatorship, economic planning, or the various partial forms of government intervention in the economic process. To attack political dictatorship is one thing; to attack a planned economy quite another; to link the two explicitly is a writer's privilege, if he can defend his thesis; and to bring every form of government control of industry into the same picture would be to fashion a political theorist's nightmare. But when Mr. Lippmann shuttles back and forth from one type of collectivism to another, treating them all as qualitatively alike and attributing—by implication—fascist brutality and militarism to the U.S.S.R. and the scope of Soviet economic planning to the mild measures of the New Deal, one can only gasp at the shambles of undistributed muddles. What Mr. Lippmann is in effect doing, whether he knows it or not, is to brand with the fascist stigma every attempt by mankind to carve out a good society for itself by conscious social action. If his book were not so confused as to be ineffective, it would be dangerous. For by presenting as the only alternatives a totalitarian dictatorship on the one hand and an individualist capitalism on the other, he consigns the future of mankind to the terribly weak props of a laissez faire economy. Since those props are certain to collapse, the final prospect we are confronted with is fascism. Actually, man's fate lies with a whole variety of socialisms and partial collectivisms that are yet unexplored.

Thus, having erected a variety of strawmen like laissez faire which he proceeded to attack, and having shown no real effort to understand the substance of *The Good Society*, Lerner now proceeded to demonstrate his animus toward free enterprise. Lippmann, he wrote, had "been able to adhere to the ideals of his liberalism and the idols of the marketplace at the same time." His thinking had "swung round under the pressure of events from the liberalism of the left to the liberalism of the right; the catchwords have remained the same, but the content is the opposite of what it was."

Mr. Lippmann's brand of liberalism is the intellectual garment of capitalist power; it is the liberalism of the Supreme Court majorities; of the business men who call for a determined muted predacity [sic]; of the professors and editors and lawyers who want at the same time to preserve the status quo and their self-respect. It is not the dishonest intellectuals who are the best servants of bankers and industrialists today. It is those who cling with the fiercest sincerity to a body of principles that represent the death's-head of capitalist power dressed up in its Sunday best.[2]

Curiously enough, both reviewers chose to ignore Secretary of Agriculture Henry Wallace's earlier observation that the New Deal's agricultural program could only be fully implemented with "the extraordinary complete control of all agencies of public opinion. . . . Complete army-like nationalist discipline in peace time," a statement that flew in the face of all the assurances by collectivist liberals that planning and democracy were not incompatible.[3]

For Harold Laski it was clear that Lippmann's positions rested

on a sophisticated reading of [Ludwig von] Mises; and it will land him, eventually, into a kind of diluted fascism. For that school of thought, believing that the "natural system of simple liberty" in industry is the best, he then begins, like Mises and Hayek, to disapprove of the institutions which hinder its functioning. The most obvious are the trade unions. They then become the critics of these and are used by the dictators to provide a philosophy of limitation on trade union power which culminates in the 'gemutlichkeit' of Austrian fascism. But what impresses me . . . is the abysses of ignorance he reveals of social processes. He really ought to be at Harvard in active alliance with Sorokin."[4]

Nothing could have better illustrated the chasm between the traditional liberalism of people like Lippmann and Pinchot, and the antifree enterprise "liberalism" of people like Lerner and their Marxist allies.

Pinchot was no great admirer of Lippmann, having expressed his reservations about the columnist both in private and in print, but he found much in *The Good Society* deserving of approval. Pinchot wrote "The Liberal Position" in the *North American Review*:

The first half of Mr. Lippmann's book is, in essence, an attack on collectivism, and by inference that is more than inference, on President Roosevelt's philosophy, and that of the men whose thinking seems to guide the government. Also it is a prophecy, buttressed by historical parallels, to the effect that our excursion into collectivism, or centrally managed economy, will prove disappointing; that it will reduce the fecundity of industry, and do away with the competitive markets which alone, Mr. Lippmann believes, can properly govern prices and the volume of production.

And finally, Mr. Lippmann contends that, having discouraged the creation of weath, reduced employment, smothered development in stultifying uniformity, and debased the standards of living, collectivism must take refuge in militarism and war.

It is from these chapters that the reader draws the conclusion that our form of government, which is democracy, and our method of enterprise, which is capitalism, form together a system which, if protected from privilege and monopoly, as Mr. Lippmann believes it can be protected, is far more effective than collectivism for increasing the general level of well-being.

Pinchot was disappointed, however, that *The Good Society* gave the impression that "in North America at least, the fight for liberalism has been waged by Mr. Lippmann all alone." He wished, too, that Lippmann had from the mass of material in the book, "set down the high points of his discussion and, more than that, indicated the deductions which might fairly be drawn from them." Since in his view Lippmann had not done so, Pinchot spelled them out, himself, thereby setting forth what he regarded as the credo of a genuine liberal:

1. Managed economy will prove undesirable. It should be abandoned. It requires a degree of discipline and control which must turn into fascism. It is restrictive and sterile. It devitalizes production and reduces the incentive for creating wealth and the expansion and differentiation of produce which alone can raise the standard of living and keep labor employed.

2. Managed economy, because it is economically impotent and conducive to under-production, tyranny and unhappiness, leads to militarism and war.

3. A government cannot effectively produce wealth. By wealth we mean the goods and services people need. Governments are not properly organized for industry. But, by statues of wide and general application, governments can lay down and enforce the rules which shall govern the industrial game. And, when this has been done, if a government is wise and mindful of its people's good, it will make itself as scarce as possible.

4. Labor and other groups cannot effectively be protected by subsidies and government-given privileges. These paralyze production and impoverish all classes.

5. Labor should be unionized for its own sake, and for industry's sake as well. And there should be responsible bargaining on both sides. But labor's main reliance for good wages and conditions of employment, and for employment itself, is the vitality and resourcefulness of industry conducted for profit.

6. Machine industry, while it brings temporary unemployment, has the long range effect of increasing employment, provided monopoly does not intervene to raise prices and reduce consumption. Dislocation of labor, on account of technological advance, is a problem that can be taken care of by private and public insurance and by work on government projects.

7. Monopoly can be prevented. And the line of attack should be that of separating the monopolist from the privilege, or privileges which give him his power to destroy competition and fix prices.

8. It is probable that good monetary control can greatly reduce the chance of major depressions, if not prevent them. The flow of money and credit should be controlled centrally. But the agencies of control should be responsible to Congress and not to the President. This point, like some of the ones I have mentioned, Mr. Lippmann adumbrates but does not actually mention.

9. A government controlled by the discretion of a ruler, or a group, is probably the ugliest and most costly phenomenon to be found in society. On the other hand, a government democratically controlled, and functioning through common council and law, is the highest and most hopeful achievement of man.[5]

The line was drawn between traditional liberals of the Pinchot and Lippmann stripe, and the collectivists who masqueraded as liberals within the Roosevelt administration and within the pages of *The New Republic* and *The Nation*.

Ekirch writes that "Even though the point of view of Lippmann's Inquiry [*The Good Society*] was hardly welcomed by New Dealers, it reflected the concern of many moderate liberals." Allen Nevins, who thought it "capital," complained that "the nasty reception it has had from much of the press is a sad reflection on the brainlessness of present-day radicalism in America. I refer to the press of the intelligentsia, so called," he added paranthetically.[6]

While controversy swirled around his book, Lippmann continued submitting both the collectivist liberals and Roosevelt to scrutiny in his nationally syndicated *New York Herald-Tribune* columns. When the economy began to slip in the second half of 1937, the columnist linked it to the collectivist ideology in the Roosevelt administration. The problem for businessmen, he wrote, was one of trying "to operate a capitalist system under a government which dislikes the system, and would, if it had the courage and power, replace it by the collectivist system." The resulting "deadlock" left business unable to go ahead "because it is terrorized by the New Dealers," and the New Dealers unable to proceed because "being only half-hearted collectivists, they do not dare to follow out the logic of their own ideas." The New Dealers would like business to become prosperous enough that it might be "milked" for the funds they could use to "finance its own gradual extinction," but business could not become prosperous without the guarantees from the administration that would give it "the security under which it can prosper." How the impasse would be resolved, Lippmann wrote, was impossible to predict, because "since we have irresponsible personal government in Washington, no one can know how Mr. Roosevelt will meet the issue."[7]

Lippmann found it remarkable that in a nation whose "economic weight and influence counts for something like a third to a half of the whole capitalist order in the world, there is an administration which disbelieves in the capitalist system," and with a president "exercising incalculable personal power, who thinks of himself not as a constitutional chief magistrate but as a specially selected leader enjoying some special and almost mystic inspiration from the subconscious wisdom of the crowd." Roosevelt, he wrote, did not possess the powers of a Mussolini or a Hitler, but he did "possess decisive personal power over the vital elements of the American economy, and . . . by training, study, experience, and natural endowment, he is not fitted to exercise that much power," and wielded it "in an entirely haphazard and unaccountable fashion," with no input from "first rate" advisers because such advisers could not "speak their real minds and still keep their places." Lippmann continued, "With the Executive's power greater than it has ever been in our whole history, the President lives not under a constitution, but as a personal sovereign surrounded by his courtiers. He seems even to have gotten around to having a court jester, which in principle would be excellent, if this jester [an obvious reference to Thomas Corcoran] did not happen also to think he was a messiah." The nation required responsible government, Lippmann wrote, not a personal government based on the "inspirations, divinations, improvisation and mystifications" of one man.[8]

The economic ignorance of a president with such powers was a matter of continuing concern also. When Lippmann looked at Roosevelt's state of the union address in January 1938, he wondered how the president's call for an increase of the national income to $90–$100 billion annually could be achieved by controlling farm surpluses and setting minimum wages. Was it "really possible that more wealth is produced by producing less wealth, or that higher prices for a smaller quantity of goods and services will result somehow in a greater quantity of goods and services?" For five years Roosevelt had confused "a different distribution of the national income with an increase in the total national income." But Roosevelt's "nonchalance" in dealing with the new economic crisis convinced Lippmann that the president had concluded it was "not worth while to try for a true revival of private enterprise, if the price is the modification of his social reforms." For political purposes the White House could always engineer a temporary and artificial recovery through massive government spending that would carry it through the November elections.[9] This was, of course, tantamount to concluding that Roosevelt was not truly interested in a business recovery that was not consistent with the collectivist objectives in and around the White House. It was a view long since reached by other columnists and traditional liberals.

Gradually, Pinchot, too, was coming to a conclusion harbored by others—that Roosevelt, or at least those around him, were not interested in recovery from the Depression. He wrote journalist Dorothy Thompson late in May: "If the administration, by deliberate sabotage or blundering, prevents an increase in production and material comfort we will, I suppose, go through the wringer [of revolution]. We shouldn't have to go through it. And I'm still inclined to think we won't. But it all depends, most of it, anyhow, on the return of prosperity which, apparently, our friends at Washington don't give a damn about—for it means an inevitable weakening of their power and an end of their primrose path."[10]

To liberal Democratic Senator Burton K. Wheeler he wrote that it had become evident many New Dealers had "reached the conclusion that it is a bad thing to have recovery proceed," since recovery would present an obstacle for carrying out their program and would "transform them from people of enormous consequence, with the destiny of millions in their hands, to everyday mortals, perhaps out of a good job.[11]

In early June he wrote to publisher Roy Howard that the New Dealers knew "that, when the people who are now unemployed and on relief become independent of government help, it will mean the end of their primrose path and perhaps the end of their jobs.[12] Business he found was not "holding its own very well against Roosevelt's constant threats and the foolish drafts of proposed bills which keep emanating from the White House in a turgid and more or less poisoning stream. I wish Roosevelt would learn that he cannot at the same time smash business and production and help labor."[13]

But Pinchot was confident that the fight over the executive reorganization bill would "tend to bust the administration." He explained to fellow progressive William Hard: "Roosevelt seems to have abandoned discretion altogether. Apparently he is under the impression that he can do any damn thing he wants to. Let us hope he will continue in that happy condition long enough to bring the desired result."[14] To Max Eastman he wrote in mid-June that he was devoting himself to preventing "the President from setting up a dictatorship" through such "sly, faking bills" as the Black–Connery Labor Bill and the Executive Reorganization Bill, and "the new A.A.A." He added, "The people who are trying to stamp out the fire which they, at least, believe to be consuming democracy have, I think, a fairly big job. Also, I think they are doing it pretty well, as shown by the result of the Court bill fight." He did not agree with Eastman that Roosevelt was "protecting capitalism," for he was convinced FDR was a "collectivist at heart." If the president did save capitalism, it would "be a fascist capitalism run by a very, very strong central power which has nothing to do with the real capitalism."[15]

After hearing a radio talk by former NRA head Hugh Johnson, Pinchot wrote publisher Roy Howard: "Whether, as Hugh Johnson thinks, Roosevelt is a sort of noble and feeble idiot, surrounded and controlled by brilliant young Machiavelis [sic] who twist him around their fingers at will, or whether he is an exceedingly ambitious and unscrupulous demagogue remains to be seen. As you know, I have for some time been inclined to the latter theory."[16]

The wave of labor violence in mid-1937, fomented by John L. Lewis and his Congress of Industrial Organizations (CIO), and supported by the Roosevelt administration, offended Pinchot, who wrote that by Roosevelt's encouragement of labor violence, the president might "be building up his political strength with Lewis's group, but he is sowing a great deal of well founded opposition to organized labor and collective bargaining." In Pinchot's view, the president "having lost a lot of support through his Court bill and other cuckoo bills . . . is now working day and night to compensate for the loss by binding Lewis and his people to him with hooks of steel." It was, Pinchot said, a case of "fairly low grade political profiteering at the long expense and discredit of organized labor." Pinchot was convinced that Roosevelt was "not unwilling to see recovery sabotaged, production and employment cut down, and a great deal of violence started so that he will have a chance to come in at the right moment and make himself extremely powerful." In Roosevelt's case, he wrote, "we have to deal with an implacable person, with an impaired sense of responsibility."[17]

To Senator Homer Bone, Pinchot wrote that it had become apparent Roosevelt believed "that the objectives or policies of the country are matters for his determination alone, and that the sole function of Congress is to find methods and set up the ways and means with which to carry out objectives which he has chosen." This amounted to "a direct attack on the theory and practice of representative government," and sought "a Congress of puppets." He asked Bone to "take a courageous and aggressive stand against personal government. Much is at stake."[18] Roosevelt's position was, he told Roy Howard, "the most complete repudiation of the theory of American government that any man has made since Alexander Hamilton in Philadelphia made his speech asking for a President with absolute veto power over the Federal and State legislatures and for a President with life tenure." He told Howard, "Every single thing the President has done since you helped reelect him has been a move toward a dictator's power."[19]

He wrote Arthur Hays Sulzberger of the *New York Times*: "As H. G. Wells pointed out, Mr. Roosevelt is implaccable. He seems devoid of all sense of responsibility or fear of the future. He is going ahead for all he's worth, like a runaway horse, till he falls or is stopped."[20]

In late July he wrote Howard again:

Mr. Roosevelt's setback will not set him back very long if the opposition lets up. His struggle to control the court will go on for the simple reason that he and his advisors want a form of society which can only be made possible with a subservient court. They will go on working day and night for such a form of society, just as long as their objectives are not made clear to the people. Every bad condition—poverty, violence, stagnation, whatever it may be—will be seized by Franklin D. and the Niebelungens (spelling slightly doubtful) to arouse the public, to mark down democracy, and to bring in an order which will give Roosevelt and his merry men power, and more power, and then some more.

These people who are quietly running the show, with, I think the full consent and approval of the President, are extremely able. They stay late at their desks. They cooperate. They have lots of money and lots of agents and a swell organization to work with. And they know what they're after and they move fast.

It is true they have made some mistakes lately and they have been spanked for them. But they will not go out of business or lose their grips on the steering gear until the country is thoroughly on to their curves.

Millions of people still believe in him as they believe in sweet Jesus. More millions are puzzled about him and slightly suspicious. But hardly anybody understands what Roosevelt and his crew are really driving for, and will go on driving for unless the country is thoroughly wised up.[21]

A few days later Pinchot addressed another public letter to Roosevelt. In it he called the president's attention to three bills the White

House had sent to Congress in 1937: the judiciary bill, the Executive Reorganization Bill, and the Black–Connery Bill. The bills, he noted, had "been altered considerably by Congress since they were submitted by you. . . . The bills in their original form cannot become law." Pinchot then continued:

Yet the original drafts—as approved by yourself—are of immense importance. They are important because, only by studying them, can the country discover where you propose to lead it. Finally, they are important since, so far as I know, they are the only authentic written record, and the only accurate description of (a) the kind of government you, and the men who drafted these bills, want to set up in this country, and (b) the degree of control, over industry and labor, you are apparently anxious to impose.

Mr. President if these bills were placed on the statute books, as they came from the White House, and sustained by a packed Supreme Court, they would throw the country into fascism in a fortnight. They would transform our economic life into a bureaucratic collectivism. In short, they would wholly change the character of government and industry, and put both under the personal domination of one man, namely yourself.

Pinchot then submitted the three bills to a searching analysis that bolstered his claim.[22]

Early in August, Pinchot wrote publisher Paul Block that it seemed "as if Roosevelt was going right ahead shoving us farther and farther toward autocracy." He explained that the president's action in "holding up the loans to the cotton growers and threatening that they would receive no loans unless Congress promised to give him . . . control of agricultural production [was] pretty sinister stuff." Roosevelt was "using the money appropriated by Congress as a means of forcing his will on Congress."[23]

Pinchot found "one of the most ironical things in the set-up is that Congress voted to the President the un-earmarked billions with which he controls and punishes Congress. Congress is like a dog that brings his whip to his master."[24] He wrote another correspondent, "One of our difficulties is that, while the President, in his speeches, mentions objectives which are most worthy in most respects, the bills which come from the White House to carry these objectives out are perfectly outlandish. But the people never see these bills. They just hear Mr. Roosevelt say that fair wages and reasonable hours of work are good for any community. And then they assume that anyone who opposes the Black–Connery wages and hours bill is a pretty cold-blooded person."[25]

By early November, however, Pinchot heard some optimism expressed by another veteran liberal. Lincoln Colcord wrote:

What encourages me is not the activity or power of the opposition, or any-thing much that can be done from the outside. But the inside is disinte-grating. Franklin D. has, I believe, gone over the emotional dam; from now on he can be trusted to tip over his own apple cart. The economic situation is closing in on him, and he doesn't know what to do about it. He says he will balance the budget and cut taxes, but he can't take business into camp on that score any longer. He can't do those two things, either. And very soon he will rip out something that spoils his new position. For his heart still lies in the direction of bust-Wall-Street reform.

I think you will find the new Congress in an ugly mood of mingled inde-pendence and chagrin. The boys will begin to look for ways to get out from under their past records, hardly knowing what they are trying to escape.[26]

Pinchot, however, was convinced that "the ideology boys" would grab Roosevelt "and pull him back into line. . . . Though Congress, since the Great Slave Rebellion, will not be so easy to handle." If any "turn in the wheel of fortune gives Roosevelt back his power, he will re-assert his technocratic and fascist–socialist schemes" unless he was "hammered."[27]

Declining in December to sign a statement of the National Un-employment League, Pinchot wrote that "the main thing that is causing unemployment today is the recession of business due to the New Deal's policies, which are so uncertain, and so hostile to production, that business does not dare expand and employ more labor." He would not sign the NUL's petition because "the drafters of the petition do not really believe in private industry or in the profit system, and, therefore, they are in another pew from me."[28] He wrote publisher Paul Block: "Here is a man who has spent thirty-seven billions and, for over four years, had more power than any President dreamed of. And what have been the results? Will labor ask itself this question? And how will it answer it?"[29]

As 1937 came to an end. Pinchot hoped for a better 1938, though he knew that "the prospects are not very bright." No assurances that Roosevelt could give business now would have any effect, "for everyone knows he cannot be believed. The only hope is that Con-gress will make him impotent."[30] Most "sane men," he wrote an-other correspondent, were "coming to the opinion that he and his little crew of wreckers will be glad to destroy capitalism and take over industry and embark on the big socialist experiment which has been at the back of their minds for a long time."[31]

When Justice Sutherland retired from the Supreme Court, open-ing the way for another Roosevelt appointment, Pinchot was "sick at heart." It meant that the nation must now "rely on Congress to scrap the insanity and puerility of New Deal economics."[32] To veteran liberal Oswald Garrison Villard, former editor of *The Nation*, Pinchot wrote in March:

I began as a New Dealer but have come to the conclusion, quite unwillingly, that Roosevelt's policy is predicated on the proposition that votes must be obtained at any cost, and by whatever series of deceptive promises may be necessary.

The President is gambling with the lives and happiness of millions of human beings in order to strengthen himself with certain groups of voters. And I don't believe he will stop even at keeping the country in depression, and perhaps forcing it into war in order to hold, and, if possible, increase his power.

Whatever may have been the sins of industrialism in the past, and whatever they may be now, this is mainly an industrial country, a business country. And for the President to promise high wages and an abundant life, and at the same time cripple industry by silly and ever-changing policies, seems to me about the limit of lack of scruple.[33]

He wrote another correspondent in April 1938, that he had "thought for some time that Mr. Roosevelt was ready to throw the country into war if he could not keep his power in any other way."[34]

The collapse of the economy late in 1937, and the onset of the "Roosevelt depression," signalled that among its other faults the New Deal had been a failure at creating genuine economic recovery. Roosevelt's gay promises that America was "On Our Way" had been exposed as empty words and failed programs. Faced with a crisis similar to that in March 1933 but having squandered the political capital he possessed then by his arrogant grasp for power in 1937, and bankrupt of new ideas, the president at first ignored the deteriorating situation as if unaware that it existed. In the special session of Congress late in 1937, Roosevelt shocked critics and supporters alike by proposing no new curatives and, instead, pursuing the course recommended by such combative counselors as Frankfurter and Laski—of trying again to push through Congress the legislative package that had been rejected during the regular session as a gauntlet to the legislators and Supreme Court over the constitutional issue. Not until the next year did Roosevelt acknowledge the collapse of the economy by asking for new relief appropriations to deal with the unemployed.

For liberal Senator Charles McNary the cause of the downturn lay in the fact that Roosevelt had "vacillated considerably in his attitude toward business. He is on one day and off the next. The uncertainty of what he will do has made business men timorous and I think has much to do with the present recession."[35] When the

White House unveiled a new spending policy to try to reverse the Roosevelt depression of 1937, Pinchot wrote; "Now we're off on a new fight against the spending and pump-priming folly."[36] He agreed with Hugh Johnson's observation that "the present big spending program was clearly a device to buy the country."[37]

To the president, Pinchot wrote that "the man who controls the money that is taken from the people in taxes is, in effect, a dictator—no matter what office he may hold, and irrespective of the form of government." The three billion dollar relief and pump-priming bill introduced in Congress on 9 May raised, he told Roosevelt, "a very great and immediate issue." Pinchot explained, "For, if this bill becomes a law, in its present form, without proper limitation upon your authority to allot and spend, it will, in all likelihood, clothe you with much of the power over the country's political and economic life, which you would have gained had the Court Packing Bill, the Black–Connery so-called Wages and Hours Bill, and the Executive Reorganization Bill all had been placed on the statute books." The bill, he concluded, would "neither bring recovery, nor reduce unemployment. It is clearly a scheme to restore White House power by buying support in the coming elections." It would "go far toward liquidating our two-party system of government by putting a faction of one party, dominated by one man, in control of the United States. The bill should be fought by every American who loves his country and honestly believes in democratic institutions." Two methods had historically been used by leaders to restore lost prestige "and make the people forget their trouble." One of these was through war, "or a war scare." "The other is to spend huge sums and make the electorate dependent on and beholden to the government. Sometimes both methods are used at once." Pinchot cited several examples of the former approach by the Roosevelt administration, including the president's "quarantine" speech in Chicago in 1937. As for the spending approach, Pinchot insisted that any money appropriated by Congress for relief belonged to the people, not to the government, and it should be allocated by the people's elected representatives, with its actual expenditure in the hands of local, nonpartisan commissions. "But giving the President and his appointees huge sums of tax money to dispose of as they please, and place here or there according to party or personal advantage, is so wrong and so unfair to those who need help, that no public servant, who is more than a politician in the less desirable sense of that word, should defend or tolerate it for a moment."

As for the "pump-priming" approach to recovery, what results had the New Deal's efforts in this respect produced since 1933? Clearly none at all. The United States was lagging behind the industrial nations of the world in its record of recovery. While many New Deal measures had "been couched in liberal language, and often prefaced with deceptive and liberal-sounding preambles, they have, in reality, been backward-looking measures. For every inch they conceded to liberalism they took us a yard toward reaction and one-man government. . . . Like the dictators of Europe, you have demanded more power as you have been given more. You have gained an ever tighter grip on government, business, labor and agriculture. Wages must be fixed by the Executive, hours must be filed. The flow of industrial production must be regulated by the government. Prices must be fixed. Our farms must be sown and reaped according to the will of Washington bureaucrats. Congress and the courts must function in fear in the far-flung shadow of the White House."[38]

In mid-June, Pinchot wrote a correspondent that he agreed "with you absolutely that Roosevelt and his close advisors are not out for real recovery, and that this charge must be made and substantiated."[39] In September, Pinchot addressed a long public letter to John L. Lewis, head of the CIO. After citing his own record in labor's support over the years, Pinchot warned Lewis that "a force profoundly hostile to labor's interests has appeared in this country for the first time." That force, he explained, was "Political Centralization . . . an all-powerful and over-ambitious federal government, which is sacrificing labor to politics—and politics to an ever-growing itch for power." The result was that the New Deal, "for all its promises and high-sounding phrases," represented "a greater threat to labor than any economic or political force that has confronted labor at any time in America's history." It's supposedly prolabor policies had, in fact brought industry to the point of paralysis, "and the birthright of American labor, which is its opportunity to find work and make a living, is being impaired." Labor's interests, Pinchot wrote, did not "lie in joining with people who are trying to force the country further and further to the left—toward political and economic dictatorship." Labor could only find security in "protecting democracy and the existing system of private enterprise," but these things were "being gradually—and none too gradually—liquidated by a strong centralized government which is falling more and more under the control of one man."[40]

— 9 —

Disenchantment

Hiram Johnson shared Pinchot's assessment of Roosevelt, writing in June 1937 that if he had harbored any doubts about Roosevelt's dictatorial ambitions, "the bills that he has thrown at us in the last few days would convince me of it. His Reorganization bill is a certain step, and a long step in that direction, while his wages and hours bill places all industry in the hands of one of his commissions.[1] When the Senate approved the Executive Reorganization Bill, Roosevelt celebrated the victory as showing that the Senate had not been swayed by the misrepresentations of the bill's opponents. Johnson regarded the president's remarks as a reflection on the Senate's members and lashed out in response. Roosevelt's attitude gave only further reason to distrust his ambitions.[2]

Late in January 1938, concerns about Roosevelt's dictatorial inclinations had reached such a point that his son denied them over national radio, and in late March the president himself roused reporters at 1 A.M. to receive a copy of a letter he had allegedly written to a friend in which he disclaimed any interest in becoming a dictator or of seeking a dictatorship in the United States.[3] Roosevelt's "night-shirt" denial of any dictatorial ambitions did not, Johnson observed, mean "a damn thing." Indeed, the fact that the issue had reached the stage of public discussion and presidential denial only demonstrated the seriousness of its dimensions, and, as Lower observes, "were themselves salutary events" in Johnson's mind. There followed the defeat of the Executive Reorganization Bill in the House of Representatives, largely over the issue of presidential power and the growing distrust in Congress of Roosevelt. The president now seemed to Johnson to be "losing his balance," and if that continued the nation might be spared dictatorship.[4]

The defeat of Roosevelt's grab for the Supreme Court, Johnson considered a "sockdolager" that had saved the United States at least temporarily from dictatorship.[5] Johnson had also voted against the administration's Wages and Hours bill, explaining to his son that he was not opposed to setting minimum wages and prescribing hours, only to placing that power in the hands of a board in Washington, which "would be one more way of turning over the economic life of the country to the President for him to exercise at his own sweet will. I decline to do this."[6]

Johnson's biographer notes that he had supported FDR in most of his domestic program during the first administration, but had, "without exception . . . opposed each new initiative in the second." Johnson, he added, had repudiated none of his beliefs between the two terms. He had repudiated only "Roosevelt and a New Deal that, for all its professions of progressivism, seemed increasingly threatening to the very progressive values he had always embraced." Johnson had become convinced that, in Lower's words, "Roosevelt built and destroyed political coalitions not to serve the nation's needs but to serve his own unquenchable ambitions."[7]

In particular, Johnson now realized the uses to which the enormous blank checks given to Roosevelt by Congress were being put by the New Dealers. Those enormous, "discretionary" appropriations had given the Roosevelt administration the power, Lower writes, "to reach beyond Congress and shape a new political landscape of constituencies that owed their allegiance to the White House," besides using it to control Congress. In short, as Pinchot had frequently pointed out, Congress had been placing in Roosevelt's hands the very whip that he used to lash them into subservience.[8]

Like Pinchot, Johnson worried that Roosevelt's domestic defeats might lead the president to embroil the nation in foreign adventures. He regarded Roosevelt's 1937 "quarantine speech" as an indication that the president "was adopting the cynical view oft expressed by Napoleon,—'when your people become restless, or irritated, or discontented, or unhappy, amuse them with a foreign war.' His naval plan would indicate that perhaps this sort of thing was running in his head."[9] But he also saw the quarantine speech as an example of "a remarkable technique that [Roosevelt] always uses, which is as old as the hills and yet constantly new. When anything arises that is disquieting he diverts the mind of the people and sets them thinking of other things." In this case, it seemed clear that the quarantine speech had been designed to take the furor over Hugo Black's KKK connections off the front pages.[10]

Johnson continued to oppose the Reorganization bill through its many amended versions, writing that it was "a companion bill to the Court bill," designed, in this case, to transfer power from Congress to the White House. Despite the fact that it had by now been so amended as to appear bland enough for some in Congress to support, Johnson still considered it "an iniquitous measure, and it is my purpose to fight it."[11] Johnson had, he told his son, "the sort of hunch that never has failed me that the Reorganization Bill is the small crack in the dike that will let through the torrent." Despite the amendments, it still contained enough "to make the President all-powerful."[12]

When even the amended bill was defeated in April, Johnson rejoiced that "the American people, for the first time, although tremors had struck them before this, felt a great fear of one man government." The original bill submitted by the president had, he told his son, given him "such tremendous power over every conceivable department, even the semi-judicial ones, that there was real cause for the fear the people had; and in addition, the midnight shirt-tail letter of the President that he did not want to be dictator added to the resentment and the fear."[13]

When New Dealer Claude Pepper won a Democratic primary election victory in Florida in May 1938, it seemed to indicate that Roosevelt and the New Deal were still popular with the people. Johnson wrote that in the changed mood of the White House—from "badly scared" to "again in command"—he would "not be surprised to see any day the Reorganization Bill again brought up." Yet Johnson noted a contrary indication of the New Deal's standing that the press had largely ignored—the crushing defeat of a pro-New Deal incumbent in South Dakota on the same day as the Florida result.[14] A few weeks later, Johnson repeated that Roosevelt had been "in a chastened mood before the Florida primary," but since then he had grown "extremely cocky, and is pursuing his role as dictator even worse than before. This spending program bodes ill for us all."[15]

Felix Morley regarded Roosevelt's appointment of Hugo Black, a steadfast New Dealer, to the Supreme Court as another "egregious blunder" by a President who "seems to me to be losing his grip."[16] The revelations of Black's life membership in the Ku Klux Klan made a caricature of Roosevelt's arguments for reform of the court, and led Morley to print a cartoon of a hooded figure on the bench with the caption "Reform of the Judiciary." Morley expected that the Black episode, combined with a new break in the stock market, would be "sure to widen the already deep fissure between Roosevelt and his opponents." The opponents, however, lacked leadership, and Morley lamented the absence of a "conservative philosophy," adding "outside of the editorial page of the Post, Dorothy Thompson and Walter Lippmann I don't see many signs that one is emerging. Probably it is the function of real Liberalism in this country to give the Conservatives a philosophy which will drive off reactionary influences. It is along that line I conceive our editorial page can be most useful."[17]

In mid-October, Morley editorialized:

There are many besides President Roosevelt who, as he puts it, "get bored sitting in Washington hearing certain people talk and talk" about the proper function of government. And one of the lines of talk that is getting more boring is the veritable complex to the effect that "enemies of democracy" or "economic royalists" or "financial oligarchs" or what-have-you are always somehow trying to do the Nation dirt.

According to their limited lights, and making due allowance for their feudal upbringing, many of these misguided fellows are really quite decent citizens. Their ideas, crude as they may seem when compared with those emanating from the fountainhead of wisdom, are often entirely sincere and sometimes not wholly vicious. It might even be the part of statesmanship, though perhaps not good stump speaking, to ease up on the rather cheap aspersions which have now come to seem inseparable from "fireside talks."

For wherever the function of government may be placed, between anarchy on the one hand and autarchy on the other, one negative conclusion about the function of a President may be confidently asserted. He is not doing credit to his job as first citizen if he habitually and deliberately baits and impugns the motives of certain minority groups among his fellow countrymen.[18]

Examining the collapse of the economy late in 1937, Morley wrote that the failure of Roosevelt's efforts to produce recovery through four years of pump priming "must be definitely linked with a reform program which in many aspects is unintelligent, unsuccessful and injurious." Those who had criticized the New Deal for its emphasis on reform over recovery had "been constantly damned as reactionaries. Abuse has been hurled at them, their motives have been questioned, and their legitimate questions drowned out by floods of shallow soapbox ridicule." But the collapse of the economy had shown "the soundness of their contentions."[19]

In the midst of the "Roosevelt Depression," Morley wrote that the economic situation offered little to be cheerful about. Meanwhile, "Roosevelt, who today put out an incredibly silly statement on his lack of desire or qualification to be a dictator, is obviously a spent force." Morley looked forward to the November congressional elections for the possibility of "some staggering changes."[20] A week later, Morley celebrated the defeat in the House of the Reorganization bill, calling it "the worst defeat for Roosevelt since the failure of the Court-packing plan, with which blunder the present outcome is intimately connected." Roosevelt was "now clearly on the defensive—the New Deal in retreat—and it may be that we shall soon have to be calling for an adequate exercise of executive authority instead of protesting too much of it." Ironically, this was happening coincident with Harold Laski "beginning his second lecture at Constitution Hall on the development of Federalism."[21]

In late August Morley welcomed FDR's defeats in the South Carolina and California primaries and was confident that his attempt to "purge" the Democratic Party of independent senators would fail in the remaining primaries, as well, but Morley worried that "any outbreak of war in Europe would completely alter the political picture here, and make a Third Term for Roosevelt not merely a possibility but a probability."[22]

Still belaboring what was clearly a dead horse by this time, Laski fired off the final word over the court issue in an October 1937 article for the *Political Quarterly*. In it Laski attacked the relevance of a 1787 constitution for an America of 150 years later that was, he said, ruled as never before by big business and finance. As for lawyers, he wrote,

Because the society was governed by a written constitution, the lawyer's outlook was pivotal in the determination of its legal habits; and for the most part, the last fifty years of American society has made the lawyers, as a social group, overwhelmingly parasitic upon big business. They were, in mental outlook, an annex of Wall Street; and when they were elevated to the Bench in recognition of their success—success being mainly measured by the scale upon which big business employed them—they took to the courts, as Mr. Justice Miller has remarked, the mental habits through which their success in private business had been achieved.

Laski added,

Because, until quite recently in American history, industry had been, as it were, the nation's politics, political parties lived almost wholly within the framework of the ideology by which business men lived. Their conceptions of social action and its possible limits were largely determined by what

businessmen thought desirable. Labour, moreover, so far as it was organized, accepted in a considerable degree the outlook of business men. It
was in that first phase of evolution under capitalism in which it had little
or no consciousness of its existence as a separate class interest needing
political expression; it thought it sufficient, like British trade unions before 1900, to bring pressure to bear upon the existing parties to secure
particular legislative objects in which it was interested. From time to time,
no doubt, the separation between reality and the party ideologies might
breed protest, even as in 1912, the revolt of the progressives. But the ever-
upward turn of American social evolution seemed always capable of restoring the traditional political equilibrium.

When, therefore, the crisis of 1929 and its aftermath revealed that the
United States had an individualistic habit of mind and, as a result, a negative state at a period when the facts called for a collectivist outlook and a
positive state, a demand for the revision of constitutional principles was
inevitable. . . . The President's purpose, courageously announced, and, at
least in part, courageously attempted, was to socialize the habits of big
business, to secure that the will of the political democracy should prevail
over the little oligarchy of business men who had made the economic power
of the United States their private empire.

To that end, he required the positive state. To that end, therefore, he required such a reorientation of constitutional principles, as would give the
necessary implications of the positive state their full recognition in the
operation of American institutions. That requirement encountered obvious difficulties. It meant the subordination of economic power to political
authority. It meant that the old habit of liberty of contract as freedom for
the business man to do what he would with his own should be read in the
new context that a President with a majority could use the State-power to
subordinate property-rights to social rights. It meant, therefore, government intervention on a large scale; it meant a new place for trade-unionism
in society; it meant the end of business autocracy in the United States.

The strain is evident in a number of ways. It is seen in the bitter conflict
between the President and the Supreme Court. It is seen in the grave
need for a centralized Federal power over commerce and labour to offset
the intense centralization of economic control under giant capitalism; it is
doubtful, at the least, whether this is obtainable in the existing distribution of functions between the Federal Government and the States. It is
seen, again, in the wholly necessary attempt by the Federal Government
to investigate and to control the great nerve centers of financial power like
the banks and the stock exchanges. . . . It is seen, also, in the vast growth,
wholly unimaginable even so recently as the Coolidge epoch, of delegated
legislation by which authority over commerce and industry is entrusted,
through the President, to a great mass of administrative commissions.
This has had, of course, the inevitable effect of increasing enormously—
though, so far, beneficently—the power of the executive in the balance of
the constitution.

In a direct way, nothing has been done to redistribute functions between the Federal Government and the States since Mr. Roosevelt took office; what has been achieved by way of cooperation has been due to the persuasive instrument of Federal aid to sorely-pressed state finances. What, how-ever, is emerging from the experience of the depression is the bankruptcy of the federal idea in the face of giant capitalism. The States are obsolete as economic and administrative units.

The President himself has said in effect that the constitution suffices for all the purposes of modern America if it is generously interpreted. The difficulty in the way of accepting that natural optimism is the profound one that all the interests of big business to-day are against the conse-quences of a generous interpretation. For, in periods of a liberal-minded Congress, that interpretation means an invasion of the economic privi-leges of big business by American democracy. The whole constitution is geared to the idea of preventing such an invasion. America has evolved the need for a positive state without evolving the institutions the positive state requires. . . . No doubt the remarkable efforts of the President have done something to make its accomplishment possible. . . . But it will take at least a generation of persistent and unyielding energy to push his effort to a successful conclusion.[23]

TNR's position vis-à-vis FDR had by now passed through a subtle change, resulting from a combination of the "Roosevelt depression" into which the nation plunged in late 1937, and a public reaction that saw declines in Roosevelt's popularity and a resurgence of con-gressional opposition, especially after sizable GOP gains in the 1938 elections. Beginning with 1939, both FDR and *TNR* were obliged to give more and more attention to international problems, and the "bungling, incompetent amateurs" of whom Bliven had written in *American Mercury*, would now be called upon to save the nation from disaster.

In early March 1938, Lippmann examined the conclusions of two economists, Gerhard Colm and Fritz Lehman, concerning the com-bined effect of high income taxes and the undistributed profits tax in producing the economic collapse of late 1937. Since their conclu-sion was that the taxes had throttled new enterprise and business expansion, the only result of retaining them would be continued "stagnation and growing unemployment" unless the administra-tion increased its own financing of business, with the inevitable result that "the government itself will be the principal banker and the principal entrepreneur." However, Lippmann refused to believe that this result was the outcome of a deliberate plan, despite the publications of New Dealers like David Cushman Coyle who had advocated just such a plan in hopes of just such a result. Later in the month, Lippmann charged that "with almost no important exception every measure [Roosevelt] has been interested in for the past five months has been on tending to reduce or discourage the production of wealth," yet without the production of wealth the New Deal could not obtain the revenue for its social purposes. Thus, Roosevelt seemed trapped in a conundrum created by the conflict between his "grudges" and his "ideals." As Lippmann put it, Roosevelt "would rather punish his enemies than realize his promises. He is more devoted to his feuds than to his programs. And he comes very near to acting like a man who would rather destroy his opponents than save himself."[24]

When Roosevelt turned again to spending in order to try to revive the economy, without adopting at the same time any ingredients of a sensible recovery program, Lippmann saw it as indicating that the president was "unwilling to liquidate the commitments and the grudges which are so alarming and so discouraging to investors and business men," that he was unwilling to revise the tax system and take other steps necessary to free private enterprise. Roosevelt was continuing "to manifest his personal hostility to business men as a class."[25]

After the Republican gains in the 1938 elections, Pinchot still did not believe that the power hungry Roosevelt would "stay down or submit without a struggle to the somewhat circumscribed role to which the elections seem to condemn him."[26] He wrote that the elections "seem to me profoundly significant of a great change in America's political philosophy. We have tried the New Deal and found that the measures intended to do good have in most cases not had the expected result." The difficulty was that there was no other way "to create recovery and employment except by stimulating industrial activity, which has not been a primary purpose of the administration. That is why labor has been so hard hit by the New Deal."[27]

In Morley's view, the 1938 primaries represented yet another in the long list of Rooseveltian defeats of 1937–1938, the failure of Roosevelt's attempt to purge his Democratic opponents over the court fight having "proved a total boomerang & the evidence of the President's slipping grip is unmistakable." Roosevelt "must now either begin the consumption of humble pie or else risk splitting the Democratic Party irrevocably in pursuit of his brand of liberalism, of which centralization and extension of Federal powers are the main ingredient." But by this time Morley found that "domestic politics are completely overshadowed by the appalling situation in Europe."[28] Even the larger-than-expected gains by the GOP in the 1938 congressional and gubernatorial elections did not deflect Morley from his concern with foreign affairs. The New Deal, in his

view, had ceased to be an issue even before those elections, and
Morley worried more thereafter about the implications of the war
for the United States and for the survival of liberal government in
this country under a wartime administration headed by Roosevelt,
since the European crisis provided a clear rationale for the president to run for an unprecedented third term in the White House.

Roosevelt's attempt to purge Democratic opponents in the 1938
primary elections was further proof for Hiram Johnson "that he
has reached such a despotic and unreasonable state of mind that
he will tolerate no man who disagrees with him at all."[29] Johnson
was delighted both by FDR's failure in the purge attempt, and by
the resurgence of the GOP in the November elections after four
successive disasters at the polls. Lower sums up Johnson's position
admirably, and with it the views of many other liberals who opposed FDR and the New Deal, when he writes that once he lost
faith in FDR's integrity, Johnson "found in Roosevelt and the New
Deal only a grotesque caricature of his own progressive vision."
The New Deal had "shifted power from Congress to the White House
[and] corrupted the political process by whetting Roosevelt's impe-
rial ambitions while providing him the means to advance those
ambitions." The result was that "Congress and its constituencies
reached out for gifts and favors, indifferent to the wider consequences of their actions. . . . The caring government Johnson had
always championed had given way to a manipulative government,
the progressive society he had hoped to see flourish was rent by
anger and social division."[30]

Johnson opposed Roosevelt's bid for a third term in 1940, but his
own campaign for reelection made it unwise to speak out against
the president lest he drive away his Democratic supporters in California. It was Roosevelt who drew the line between them, telling a
press briefing in August that his affection for the Senator remained
strong, but that Johnson was no longer a liberal. Typically, Johnson
struck back, saying, "Had I followed him in his attempted packing
of the Supreme Court and his veiled and un-American deeds leading us down the road to war and dictatorship, I would have been a
perfect liberal and progressive, and what glory would be mine. . . .
This is just the same old purge, the same old sham expressions of
regards and affections, the same old stiletto."[31]

When Johnson swept to a smashing victory in both the Democratic and Republican primaries in September, ex-New Deal brain-
truster Raymond Moley wrote the following in *Newsweek*:

Early in August the President of the United States, telling the voters of
California not to return Hiram Johnson to the Senate, said that he did not

think that anyone in his wildest dreams could regard Senator Johnson as a liberal or progressive Democrat in the year 1940. Well, 483,328 Democrats had just such wild dreams—which was more than all the assorted Democrats and others who opposed Johnson could gather together. Republicans—581,858 of them—had wild dreams too. In thirty years of victory Hiram Johnson has never enjoyed such a vote of confidence.[32]

In subsequent speeches and statements, however, FDR and Johnson ignored each other's reelection bids, except for a nationally broadcast speech in mid-October. In that speech, Johnson criticized the president for violating the two-term tradition in American politics, arguing that its abandonment meant the elimination of an essential safgeguard of democracy.[33] And both won in 1940. When Roosevelt was reelected in 1940, Johnson wrote of the third inauguration of his concern that it might be the last. The Lend–Lease Law he viewed only as another Rooseveltian grasp for dictatorial power under the guise of an emergency.[34]

In January 1939 Henry Hazlitt reviewed Laski's latest book, *Parliamentary Government in England*, for the *New York Times Book Review*. The book was not, Hazlitt pointed out, a description of the workings of the parliamentary government in England but rather "for much of its length, a passionate tract devoted to hammering again and again on a single thesis. This thesis is that parliamentary democracy is incompatible with capitalism, and one or the other must be abolished." Hazlitt quoted Laski:

The maintenance of capitalist democracy means, in the long run, the transformation of capitalism into socialism by the methods democracy places at the disposal of the masses. . . . A political democracy seeks, by its own inner impulses, to become a social and economic democracy. It finds the road thereto barred by the capitalist foundations upon which the political democracy is built. . . . The House of Commons will always be able to do its work adequately so long as capitalism is able to satisfy the demands of the masses. It is . . . no longer able to satisfy them. That is what is meant by economic crisis, the prospect of war, the growth of fascism and the immense social conflicts to which these have led. It has, therefore, either to abdicate or to fight; on the evidence, the latter alternative seems the more likely.

Clearly, the content of Laski's polemic offered little that was new from his works of the early 1930s. Hazlitt added his observation:

It is not going too far to say . . . that Mr. Laski's whole attitude, which he shares with many other Marxists, is calculated to provoke the very "class war" he affects to predict. In the international field we have learned what to call this. It is known as jingoism. It is the jingo who tells us solemnly that war with this or that other country is "inevitable," that the foreign enemy intends to strike us soon or late, that we must give the most sinister interpretation meanwhile to everything he does, and that it might even perhaps be better for us (in self-defense, of course) to strike the first blow. In addition to the international war jingo we now have the class war jingo. Mr. Laski, for all of his suavity of phrase, frequently puts himself in the present volume in that class.

Finally, though it is essential to the force of Mr. Laski's argument to assume that capitalism is unworkable, unjust and wicked, and that socialism is but another name for economic heaven, he does not pause to argue either of these propositions, but in effect takes them for granted. His political thesis is based on his economics; but while he knows his politics, his economics is no more than a series of specious phrases, the stereotype of orthodox Marxist rhetoric, and his beautiful superstructure rests on quicksand.[35]

Laski and Roosevelt continued to see much of each other in 1938, but by now there was little for either of them to gain from the association, even if they did know it.[36] Ever the sycophant, Laski asked FDR for permission to dedicate a little book composed of six lectures at the University of Indiana to him.[37] Roosevelt wrote Laski to thank him for his "delightful note," and added, "Yes, do please come and see me as soon as you get back East—and, of course—I shall be honored and happy to have you dedicate the little book to me."[38] Later in the month, Roosevelt responded to a copy of an essay Laski had written on his *Public Papers and Addresses* that he wished "much it could be reprinted in some magazine with a million circulation. But such a magazine would not dare to publish it. . . . Come and see me as soon as you get East."[39]

In March 1939, Laski wrote FDR:

We leave Seattle for California on Tuesday; and I do not want to go before putting on paper two things. The first is my sense that the power projects in Washington are amongst the most exciting things I have ever seen. Whatever else happens, these remain monuments aere perennius to an administration that has been as creative as any in modern American history. Who owns power owns the future in America; and Coulee will remain in my mind as one of the supreme achievements of creative imagination in the disposition of human fortunes.

The other is the conviction that not all the railing of the good and great touches your hold here on the allegiance of the common man. There is a pretty bad machine in the North-West, and it does not do you justice. But the common man has penetrated behind its blunders and its narrowness to his sense of your purposes; and the greater the determination you show to go on with the fight, the more certain you can be of his response. . . . Other things being equal, Frida and I hope to get to Washington on the

7th of May and stay until the 11th. I hope you will have a free hour then when we can come and salute you.

In this grim and ugly world, you cannot easily imagine what a comfort your presence in the White House means to me. Let the dogs bark; you know that the caravan passes on.[40]

In mid-August, Laski wrote the president about the European situation, and added,

I have written a book on the Presidency which, maintaining all the proper spirit of what the professors call "objectivity" will, I hope, make your enemies furiously angry. Few things are more pleasant than to write a book in the guise of a scientific treatise. You may like to know that I found the "Public Papers" illuminating in grasping the technique of the process at almost every turn.[41]

In September, after the outbreak of war in Europe, Laski wrote FDR that he hoped the United States could stay out, but "it is more than ever vital to go on full steam ahead with the New Deal. The more the United States now can show successful results in the working of democracy, the greater the part it can play in the making of a new revolution of world direction. I can not think of a greater contribution to peace than this, the greater because the Soviet Union has, I fear, committed one of the supreme psychological blunders of history . . . it has thrown away an initiative which would have enabled it to share in the moral leadership of the world. Now I see no prospect of truth in its good faith for a long period to come."[42]

The prospect of collectivism in America, on which Laski had pinned such hopes early in the New Deal, was never realized. The United States seemed no closer to socialism than it had been under Hoover. Yet Laski found positive accomplishments when he looked back upon it late in 1939.

The New Deal, whatever may be its defects, has made the man in the street recognize that the State is, for good or ill, a positive instrument by whose activities the contours of his life are set. . . . The importance of that consciousness is scarcely capable of exaggeration. It sets up new standards for the activity of government. It ends the epoch of laissez-faire. It makes millions feel that when economic disaster comes, it is as natural to look to government for helpful intervention as it is to expect it to deal with a tidal wave in Galveston, or a hurricane in New England. Whatever be the mistakes of the New Deal, it has lifted the political mind of America to a new and higher level. It has had an educational significance it will be difficult not to emulate in the coming years. It has demonstrated that the processes of government are not merely important but also interesting to those who live by their results.

Moreover, the Roosevelt administration had

the Cabinet apart, brought a remarkable host of able men to Washington. It is notable that they are mostly lawyers. They have been (as the Cabinet has never been) the effective foundation of the New Deal. They have brought to it qualities that make their work of outstanding significance. . . . Certainly anyone who has seen Mr. Justice Douglas at work in the Securities and Exchange Commission, or the famous pair, Mr. Corcoran and Mr. Cohen, or Mr. Messersmith in the State Department, or Mr. E. W. Rice in Agriculture and Mr. Lubin in Labor, will have known at once that he has seen in them the qualities both of mind and heart, that can make even a governmental system as cumbrous as that of America fulfill great purposes in a great way. And they have only been leading figures in an army the quality of which proves how the drama of democratic government, once it has great ends to fulfill, can call forth ability that no other system can rival.

Laski did not explain who was responsible for the appointment of a cabinet that even he recognized fell short of the desired level of competence.[43]

We may take the publication of *The American Presidency* in 1940 as Laski's final significant attempt to influence the direction of American liberalism. The book was based on the six lectures he delivered at Indiana University in 1939, and was dedicated to Roosevelt. In a preview of the book that he wrote for the *Saturday Review of Literature*, Laski wrote of a president newly reelected to office that

he starts with important advantages if he knows how to capitalize them. For five months before his election he has been the central figure in the public attention. He has the opportunity to create expectancies. He has the power to compel discussion. What he has to say, the very minutiae of his personality, will be the theme of talk in twenty million homes. Around him and his plans are a myriad hopes and fears. His problem is to maintain all he can of the tempo of those months. . . . The experience of the New Deal has shown . . . what an immense impact the personality of a president can make when he is able to arouse and retain the conviction that something of real importance is afoot. Whatever his effect upon Congress, a president who can get to the multitude will seize the attention of the multitude. His ideas, his policies, his purposes, will shape the mental climate as will those of no other man in America. . . . What . . . is important is to emphasize this reservoir of energy to which an appeal is possible, the certainty, when it is aroused, that it will give to the president an authority over public opinion sufficient to make his purposes compete successfully with all other elements in the national life.

Power, no doubt, is always a dangerous thing; and the temptation to its abuse, as no generation has learned more surely than our own, the subtlest poison to which a man my succumb. Yet power is also opportunity, and to face danger with confidence is the price of its fulfilment. That is why I end with the emphasis that the president of the United States must be given the power commensurate to the function he has to perform. It must be given democratically; it must be exercised democratically; but, if he is to be a great president, let us be clear that it must be given. For great power alone makes great leadership possible; it provides the unique chance of restoring America to its people.[44]

The book was greeted with enthusiasm by radical reviewers in the United States, but ex-New Dealer Raymond Moley found much to question in *Newsweek*. Moley first of all found it timely that it appeared in the midst of Roosevelt's campaign for reelection, and when combined with "the unbounded admiration it displays for President Roosevelt, makes it a kind of campaign document." Moley went on:

The essence of the Laski plea is that the American President needs power, and yet more power. "Great power makes great leadership possible," he says. As for the nation, it must, if it would "live creatively . . . discipline itself to trust, in the grand manner, the leaders of its choice." So here we are! No doubt it is creative living that the Indians in every South American dictatorship enjoy. The only distinction involved seems to be that, according to the Laski prescription, the "grand manner" characterizes people who give up their power to a leader and does not characterize people when someone takes their power away from them. Still, the nation ends up in precisely the same place. . . . Since he invites us to place ourselves quietly in the hands of a leader, we have the right to ask where Laski would like to have the leaders take us. In 1935 he told us in his book, *The State*: "Once more we can see before us the beginnings of a new order. Once more the economic process has become incompatible with the political forms in which it is contained." So it would seem that we need more power in the hands of the leader because we are going to have a new order. Professor Laski elaborated his thesis last year at the University of Wisconsin: "Should war be forced upon us and we see the old, ugly, imperialist aims dominating the rulers of the democracies, we of the Labor party and the working class everywhere see it as our duty to turn those wars into civil wars and remake those governments which disregard the working classes which are their foundations."

Moley concluded that Laski's program was one that would not appeal to many Americans, since they neither believed that the economic system had become incompatible with the political system in which it existed, nor were they willing to accept a "new order" in the form of a dictatorship that masqueraded as a democracy. Even less were they willing to launch a civil war while fighting a war with another nation.[45] Thus did a traditional American liberal reject the collectivist and statist liberalism at the end of the 1930s.

Epilogue

Even such close and critical observers of the New Deal as Amos Pinchot and Hiram Johnson did not detect the subtle but noteworthy shift in the New Deal beginning with 1935. In its two characteristics that most concerned them, in fact, the New Deal did not change. These were its antibusiness orientation, and its apparent grasp for dictatorial power. Moreover, just as there had been Brandeisian elements in the collectivist early stage of the New Deal, so too, were there collectivist bills sent to Congress from the White House after 1935 which further obscured the shift.

Yet, as Ekirch has pointed out of the second New Deal: "By spending, by taxing, and by borrowing, the New Deal was [now] in effect achieving a peaceful revolution without apparent changes in the political or economic structure." Put simply, the trend now was in the direction of the use of spending and taxation to manage the economy, a la Brandeis and Coyle, rather than the collectivist planning advocated by Tugwell, Frankfurter, and Laski.[1] Absent, however, was the break-up of large industries, as was inevitably to be the case in a deteriorating international situation that offered the prospect those large industries would be needed.

The new direction was apparent to the collectivists, but they could do little else than agonize over it. The traditional liberals had flexed their muscles in the battle over the Supreme Court, and the president's freedom of action with respect to Congress died a quick death thereafter. Suspicions of FDR's motives and objectives, inflamed by that and other grabs for power, made it impossible now to enact even a moderate program of liberal reforms. As Corcoran later recalled, after the Court fight "the administration's domestic program lost momentum that it would never regain."[2]

In 1938 Walter Lippmann set out to account for the sudden and dramatic plummet of the New Deal in public favor after Roosevelt's apparent landslide victory just two years earlier. Lippmann began by pointing out that Roosevelt's victory in 1936 had not, in fact, been significantly greater than those by Harding, Coolidge, and Hoover in terms of popular votes. It was the fact that FDR had won the electoral votes of every state but Maine and Vermont that had encouraged an "optical illusion, which made it seem as if Mr. Roosevelt had been elected by acclamation and that the opposition had been annihilated. Spell-bound by this optical illusion, Mr. Roosevelt jumped to the unwarranted conclusion that he had a personal mandate from the people to reconstruct American society." Alas, a great many collectivist liberals had leaped to the same conclusion and had encouraged the president in that belief. The actions that flowed from this "optical illusion," including the attempt to pack the Supreme Court, led to the reaction exemplified by the 1938 elections.[3]

The forward progress of the New Deal substantially ended after the 1938 elections, even though Roosevelt and the radicals around him refused for some time to accept the rebuke of the American electorate. Eventually, however, the obstacles posed by the coalition of Republicans and conservative Democrats to sweeping new legislation, and the dissension within the New Deal of prominent members like Secretary of the Treasury Henry Morgenthau, made the realities apparent even to the president. Beginning in 1939 the deteriorating situation abroad made it possible for Roosevelt to turn his restless energies to foreign affairs and to abandon his fruitless war with American business.

Thomas Corcoran later recalled in his unpublished memoirs that Roosevelt had been "saved" by Adolf Hitler, without whom the president could not have shifted the economy into higher gear through war production. Hitler, Corcoran observed, furnished Roosevelt with the "immensely useful specter of a common enemy to eclipse the spectacle of his own defeat on the homefront."[4]

In November 1939, *TNR* celebrated its twenty-fifth anniversary with a special issue and a cocktail party. Invited to the party, thrown by what *Time* magazine called "the pinko weekly," were Freda Kirchwey, editor of *The Nation*, "the rival (seventy-four-year-old) liberal intellectual journal that looked exactly like *The New Republic* to outsiders, very different to liberal intellectuals," and also "contributors, constant readers, free traders, isolationists, progressive educators, single taxers, practicing Marxists, disillusioned Marxists, poets, professors, publishers, all who believe themselves to be liberals, all who thus claim to fit into a category that nobody has satisfactorily defined."

Of 1939 liberalism, *Time* opined:

As a practical political program, modern liberalism is crammed to overflowing with the souvenirs of old minority causes—distrust of big business, inherited from the trust-busters and western populists, and newly polished by Marxists; fear of political corruption, handed down by the muckrakers. And liberals, now as 25 years ago, generally hold to the right of labor to organize, and watch for violations of civil liberties. But more & more liberals have found Communists initiating movements, unearthing scandals, doing more & more of the drudgery of reform, while liberals merely passively approved, passively disapproved.[5]

The influence of Harold Laski on American liberalism in the 1930s was profound. Arthur Schlesinger, Jr., has written of Laski that "through his writings, his personal relations, and his American visits, [he] had the greatest effect on American left-wing thought in the thirties." His network of contacts had begun during his Harvard years, 1916–1920, and included Frankfurter, Holmes, Brandeis, Herbert Croly, and Walter Lippman, while he also became a contributor to *TNR* at that time. Schlesinger writes that the "elegance of his writing, his graceful notes of regret for the doomed past, his brave acceptance of the inevitabilities of the future, his poses of romantic despair and hope—all this gave him an influence in the United States far beyond that of any Marxist. And his personality—the kindliness to the poor and defenseless, the wide-ranging sympathy, the fascinating if often far too fanciful accounts of his influence on great events—further increased his American appeal. If Dewey, Beard, and Niehbuhr were the mentors of a native American radicalism, it was appropriate that a European should be the missionary of Marxism to the American infidels."[6]

In a review that he wrote of the *Holmes–Laski Letters* for the *New York Times Book Review* in February 1953, ex-New Dealer Adolf Berle observed of Laski, "With his American friends he was part of the bitter process which split the American liberal movement, as it had split the British labor movement, leading some astray in bitter climaxes whose echoes are not yet stilled." Berle recalled that when Laski died in March 1950, "some of his left-wing friends in New York proposed a memorial meeting in The

New School for Social Research, [but] there was objection from liberals; Laski had intrigued against and insulted some, and set loose extremist currents. Some said he had betrayed the faith."[7]

The truth was, however, that many American liberals had betrayed their own faith by embracing Laski's collectivist ideas, and had thereby contributed to the inability of either liberals of the New Deal to develop a consistent and coherent program for dealing with the Depression, thus contributing to the delay in recovery and to the misfortunes of millions of Americans between 1933 and 1941, perhaps even to the tragedy of World War II.

Notes

INTRODUCTION

1. James P. Young, *Reconsidering American Liberalism* (Boulder, Colo., 1996), 172–173.

2. Ibid., 173.

3. *The New Republic*, 12 June 1935.

4. Young, 176–177.

5. Thomas G. Corcoran memoirs, "Credo," 33, Thomas G. Corcoran Papers and Memoirs, Library of Congress.

6. Ibid., "Pack," C4.

7. Arnaud Dandieu, "Harold Laski—Political Philosopher," *Living Age* 339 (November 1930): 267–270. Reprinted from *Nouvelles Litteraires*.

8. Quoted in Arthur Ekirch, *Ideologies and Utopias* (Chicago, 1969), 189.

9. Herbert Croly, *The Promise of American Life* (New York, 1909).

10. Young, 177.

11. Tugwell quoted in the *Washington Post*, 28 January 1934; Isaac Lippincott, *Sold Out* (New York, 1936), vii, xii, 126.

12. Edmund Wilson, *The Thirties* (New York, 1980), 338.

13. Corcoran, "credo," Corcoran Papers, 31.

14. Theodore J. Lowi, *The End of Liberalism* (New York, 1979), 273–274.

15. Ekirch, 27–28.

16. Frankfurter to Soule, 2 June 1931, Felix Frankfurter Papers, Library of Congress.

17. Ekirch, 77–78.
18. Memorandum of meeting on 27 May 1935, Frankfurter Papers.
19. Ekirch, 137–138.
20. Ibid., 138.
21. Hallgren quoted in ibid., 206.

CHAPTER 1

1. Bruce Bliven, *Five Million Words Later* (New York, 1970), 238.
2. Ibid., 240.
3. Bliven oral history, Columbia Oral History Collection.
4. Soule to Tugwell, 14 January 1932, Rexford Tugwell Papers, Franklin D. Roosevelt Presidential Library.
5. Rexford Tugwell, "The Principle of Planning and the Institution of Laissez Faire," *Supplement to the American Economic Review* 32 (March 1932): 75–92.
6. David Seideman, *The New Republic: A Voice of Modern Liberalism* (New York, 1986), 109.
7. Gordon Greb, "7 Million Words Later: An Interview with Bruce Bliven," *San Jose Studies* 2, 2: 62–73.
8. Quoted in Gary Dean Best, *Nickle and Dime Decade* (Westport, Conn., 1991), 2.
9. Thomas G. Corcoran autobiography, Chapter 4, p. 1, Corcoran Papers.
10. Max Ascoli, "Notes on Roosevelt's America," *Atlantic*, June 1934, 655.
11. Seideman, 111.
12. Hoover to John Callan O'Laughlin, 23 August 1941, John Callan O'Laughlin Papers, Library of Congress.
13. Quoted in Andrew Berman, *We're In The Money* (New York, 1971), 116; Frankfurter to Walter Lippman, 15 March 1993, Frankfurter Papers, for Lippmann's views see Lippmann to Felix Frankfurter, 3 March 1933, ibid.
14. Thomas Tweed, *Gabriel Over the White House* (Garden City, N.Y., 1933), 85, 103.
15. Ibid., 121, 126.
16. *New York Evening Post*, 10 February 1933.
17. *New York World Telegram*, 10 February 1933.
18. Ian Hamilton, *Writers in Hollywood* (New York, 1990), 124.
19. Quoted in *Literary Digest*, 22 April 1933, 13.
20. Early to William Daley, 10 May 1933, Franklin Delano Roosevelt Papers, Franklin D. Roosevelt Presidential Library, PPF 73; FDR to William Hearst, 1 April 1933, Roosevelt Papers, PPF 62, Roosevelt Presidential Library.
21. Berman, 117.
22. *New York World Telegram*, 10 April 1933.
23. *The Nation*, 26 April 1933, 482–483.
24. *The New Republic*, 19 April 1933, 282.
25. Seideman, 112.
26. Ibid., 112–113.

27. Bliven to Frankfurter, 29 July 1933, Frankfurter Papers.

28. "Can America Spend Its Way into Recovery?" *Redbook*, December 1934.

29. Sara Alpern, *Freda Kirchwey, A Woman of The Nation* (Cambridge, Mass., 1987), 103.

30. Ibid., 104.

31. Ibid., 105.

32. Ibid.

33. Pinchot to Freda Kirchwey, 16 April 1933, Amos Pinchot Papers, Library of Congress.

34. Pinchot to Kirchwey, 24 April 1935, ibid.

35. Pinchot to George Foster Peabody, 13 January 1933, ibid.

36. Pinchot to Homer Bone, 15 February 1933, ibid.

37. Pinchot to Allen McCurdy, 22 March 1933, ibid.

38. Pinchot to Roy Howard, 3 April 1933, ibid.

39. Pinchot to Francis Heney, 20 April 1933, ibid.

40. Pinchot to Narcissa Swift, 4 May 1933, ibid.

41. Pinchot to Allen McCurdy, 16 May 1933, ibid.

42. Gardner to Pinchot, 18 July 1933, ibid.

43. Pinchot to Heney, 4 August 1933, ibid.

44. Pinchot to Ben Lindsay, 5 August 1933, ibid.

45. Pinchot to Mitchell Kennerly, 31 August 1933, ibid.

46. Pinchot to Howard, 26 September 1933, ibid.

47. Pinchot to Lewis Frissell, 23 November 1933, ibid.

48. Pinchot to FDR, 26 April 1934, ibid.

49. Pinchot to FDR, 28 June 1934, ibid.

50. Pinchot to David Stern, 11 August 1934, ibid.

51. Pinchot to Fairchild, 20 September 1934, ibid.

52. Pinchot to Fairchild, 10 November 1934, ibid.

53. Pinchot to Norbeck, 11 March 1935, ibid.

CHAPTER 2

1. Felix Morley Journal, 18 June 1934, Felix Morley Papers and Journal, Hoover Presidential Library.

2. Ibid., 5 March 1934.

3. *Washington Post*, 21 March 1934.

4. Ibid., 29 March 1934.

5. Ibid., 10 April 1934.

6. Ibid., 6 April 1934.

7. Ibid., 27 March 1934.

8. See, for example, ibid., 6 April 1934.

9. Ibid., 5 April 1934.

10. Ibid., 25 March 1934.

11. Ibid., 7 April 1934.

12. Ibid., 13 April 1934.

13. Morley Journal, 30 May 1934.

14. *Athens Daily Times*, 9 May 1934; *Atlanta Constitution*, 9 May 1934.

15. Morley Journal, 2 June 1934.

16. Ibid., 18 June 1934.

17. Ibid., 17 July 1934.

18. Ibid., 6 August 1934.

19. *Washington Post*, 30 July 1934.

20. Soule to Frankfurter, 3 May 1931, Frankfurter Papers, Library of Congress.

21. Frankfurter to Amos Pinchot, 7 July 1933, Pinchot Papers, Library of Congress.

22. Ascoli, "Notes on Roosevelt's America," *Atlantic*, June 1934, 663.

23. *New York Herald-Tribune*, 6 March 1936.

24. Ibid, 3 April 1934.

25. Cohen and Corcoran to Frankfurter, 18 June 1924, Frankfurter Papers.

26. *New York Herald-Tribune*, 4 January 1936.

27. *Washington Post*, 5 January 1936.

28. *New York Herald-Tribune*, 4 January 1936.

29. Lippmann to Newton Baker, 22 January 1936, Newton Baker Papers, Library of Congress.

30. Omaha *World Herald*, 5 January 1936.

31. Ibid., 28 January 1936.

32. *New York Herald-Tribune*, 2 July 1936.

33. Johnson to sons, 12 March 1933, in *The Diary Letters of Hiram Johnson, 1917–1945*, ed. Robert E. Burke (New York, 1983).

34. Ibid., 19 March 1933.

35. Ibid., 1 April 1933.

36. Couzens to McNary, 5 October 1934, Charles McNary Papers, Library of Congress.

37. Richard Coke Lower, *A Bloc of One* (Stanford, 1993), 269.

38. Lower, 271.

39. Burke, 4 June 1933.

40. Ibid., 16 June 1933.

41. Ibid., 2 June 1934.

42. Ibid., 26 January 1935.

43. Ibid., 10 March 1935.

44. Lower, 282–283.

45. Ibid., 284–285.

46. Burke, 29 June 1935.

47. Ibid., 21 July 1935.

48. McNary to James Couzens, 14 August 1934, McNary Papers.

49. Couzens to McNary, 23 August 1934, ibid.

CHAPTER 3

1. Harry Shulman, "Memorandum of Talk with L.D.B[randeis]—December 8, 1933," in Frankfurter Papers.

2. For recognition of Frankfurter's role as a Laski conduit to the White House see Felix Morley's observation in his review of Laski's *The Rise of*

Liberalism (*Washington Post*, 23 September 1936), that the book was important for Americans because Laski's "influence on the Roosevelt Administration, exercised in part through his own writings, and in part through Felix Frankfurter, has been very much greater than is generally realized." Also, William Yandell Elliott in *The Southern Review*, wrote of Laski that, "Through Felix Frankfurter, his influence on the Roosevelt administration has been far from negligible." William Y. Elliott, "The Modern State: Karl Marx and Mr. Laski," *The Southern Review* 1 (1935): 209–223.

3. Frankfurter to Coyle, 12 May 1932, Frankfurter Papers.

4. Coyle to Frankfurter, 16 May 1932 and 3 June 1922; Frankfurter to Coyle, 4 June 1932, ibid.

5. Coyle, *The Irrepressible Conflict* (New York, 1932), 6–7.

6. Ibid, 15.

7. Ibid., 18–19.

8. Ibid., 29–30.

9. Ibid., 34.

10. Ibid., 42–43.

11. "Harold Laski: As His Secretary Saw Him," by Ruth Meyer, with Meyer to LeHand, 9 November 1940, in FDR Papers, PPF.

12. Arthur Schlesinger, *The Politics of Upheaval* (Boston, 1960), 171.

13. Louis D. Brandeis to Elizabeth Brandeis Raushenbush, 8 April 1926, *Letters of Louis Brandeis* (New York, 1978), V, 215.

14. Edmund Wilson, *The Thirties* (New York, 1980), 338.

15. In *The Dangers of Obedience and Other Essays* (London, 1930).

16. Laski, *Democracy in Crisis* (New York, 1969 reprint), 184–185, 189–190, 211–213; 215, 217, 241, 259, 263.

17. Ibid., 259, 263.

18. Laski to Frankfurter, 12 November 1932, Frankfurter Papers.

19. Laski, "Roosevelt the Fighter," *Living Age* 343 (1933): 385–388.

20. Laski to Frankfurter, 13 August 1933, Frankfurter Papers.

21. Laski, "The Roosevelt Experiment," *Atlantic*, February 1934, 143.

22. Laski, "Freedom in Danger," *Yale Review*, March 1934.

23. Laski, "The Challenge of Our Times," *American Scholar*, October 1934, 387–399.

24. Laski to Frankfurter, 17 February 1935, Frankfurter Papers.

25. *Politica*, February 1935.

26. *New York Times*, 23 March 1935.

27. Ibid., 20 April 1935.

28. Reprinted in *Living Age*, August 1935, 554.

29. *The New Republic*, 10 April 1935.

30. Ibid., 27 November 1935.

31. Quoted in William McDonald, "Mr. Laski Takes the State Apart," *New York Times Book Review*, 24 March 1935.

32. William Y. Elliott, "The Modern State: Karl Marx and Mr. Laski," *The Southern Review* 1 (1935): 209–223.

33. Laski to Frankfurter, 23 November 1935, Frankfurter Papers.

34. Ascoli, "Retreat from Liberalism," *The New Republic*, 10 April 1935, 249.

CHAPTER 4

1. Laski to Frankfurter, 28 May 1935, ibid.
2. Laski to Frankfurter, 5 June 1935, ibid.
3. Laski to LeHand (FDR's secretary), 6 June 1935, FDR Papers, PPF.
4. FDR to Harold Laski, 18 November 1935, ibid.
5. Laski to LeHand, 14 January 1936, and LeHand to Laski, 24 January 1936, ibid.
6. McIntyre to Laski, wire, 15 April 1936, ibid.
7. Laski to Frankfurter, December 1935 or January 1936, ibid.
8. Laski to LeHand, 11 January 1936, FDR Papers, PPF.
9. *The New Republic*, 1 January 1936.
10. Ibid., 26 February 1936.
11. Landis to Frankfurter, 6 June 1936, Frankfurter Papers.
12. Franfurter to Landis, 9 June 1936, ibid.
13. Landis to Frankfurter, 6 July 1936, ibid.
14. Cardozo to Laski, 18 June 1936, Harold Laski Papers, Syracuse University.
15. Laski to Frankfurter, 18 October 1936, Frankfurter Papers.
16. Copy of Laski to Irving, St. Louis *Post-Dispatch*, undated, ibid.
17. Walter Lippmann, *New York Herald-Tribune*, 8 February 1936.
18. Ibid., 13 July 1935.
19. FDR to Norman Hapgood, 10 July 1935, FDR Papers, PPF.
20. *New York Herald-Tribune*, 18 July 1935.
21. Walter Lippmann, Omaha *World Herald*, 29 January 1936.
22. *New York Herald-Tribune*, 23 April 1936.
23. Bliven to Charles Beard, 23 June 1936, Beard Papers, Library of Congress.
24. Seideman, 126.
25. *The New Republic*, 24 June 1936.
26. Bruce Bliven, "Walter Lippmann and National Government," in ibid. 23 September 1936, 180–181.
27. Alpern, 106.
28. Ibid., 107.
29. Ibid., 108.
30. Pinchot to Ralph Flanders, 14 March 1935, Pinchot Papers.
31. Pinchot to Flanders, 16 April 1935, ibid.
32. Pinchot open letter of 16 April 1935, ibid.
33. Owen to Pinchot, 18 April 1935, ibid.
34. Howe to Pinchot, 21 April 1935, ibid.
35. Cravath to Pinchot, 23 April 1935, ibid.
36. Carl Thompson to Pinchot, 24 April 1935, ibid.
37. Pinchot to members of Congress, 7 May 1935, ibid.
38. Pinchot to FDR, 7 June 1935, ibid.
39. Pinchot to Malcom Mollan, 13 May 1935, ibid.
40. Pinchot to Richard Childs, 12 June 1935. ibid.
41. Pinchot to Thomas Finletter, 14 April 1935, ibid.
42. Pinchot to Borah, 7 June 1935, ibid.

43. Pinchot to Lewis Haney, 13 June 1935, ibid.
44. Pinchot to Kenneth B. Walton, 19 June 1935, ibid.
45. Pinchot to Walton, 26 June 1935, ibid.
46. Gannett to Pinchot, 18 June 1935, ibid.
47. Pinchot to Gannett, 26 June 1935, ibid.
48. Shaw to Pinchot, 23 July 1935, ibid.
49. *Chicago Tribune*, 24 July 1935.
50. Henry Morgenthau Diary, 24 July 1935, Roosevelt Presidential Library.
51. Pinchot to R. B. Comstock, 7 August 1935, Pinchot Papers.
52. Pinchot to Henry Moskowitz, 9 August 1935, ibid.
53. Pinchot to George Foster Peabody, 9 August 1935, ibid.
54. Pinchot to Ivan Merrick, 30 August 1935, ibid.
55. Pinchot to James Cromwell, 6 September 1935, ibid.
56. Pinchot to Francis J. Henry, 11 January 1936, ibid.
57. Pinchot to Roy Howard, 3 August 1936, ibid.
58. Pinchot to Howard, 21 May 1936, ibid.
59. Pinchot to Howard, 17 June 1936, ibid.
60. Pinchot to John Sinclair, 15 July 1936, ibid.
61. Pinchot to Harold Ickes, 14 October 1936, ibid.
62. Holmes to Pinchot, 20 October 1936, ibid.
63. Flanders to Pinchot, 16 October 1936, ibid.
64. Maurice Williams to Pinchot, 19 October 1936, ibid.
65. Cook to Pinchot, 21 October 1936, ibid.
66. Ickes to Frankfurter, 2 November 1936, Frankfurter Papers.

CHAPTER 5

1. David Cushman Coyle, "Necessary Changes in Public Opinion in the New Social Order," *National Conference of Social Work*, 1933, 38–40.
2. David Cushman Coyle, "Public Works, A New Industry," *Atlantic Monthly*, December 1933, 756–763.
3. Schlesinger, *The Politics of Upheaval*, 232–235.
4. Ibid., 193–194.
5. David Cushman Coyle, "Illusions Regarding Revolution," *Survey* 70 (July 1934): 211–214.
6. David Cushman Coyle, "Recovery and Finance," *Virginia Quarterly Review* 10 (October 1934): 481–501.
7. David Cushman Coyle, "Decentralized Industry," *Virginia Quarterly Review* 11 (July 1935): 321–338.
8. Copy of Hapgood to Louis Brandeis, in FDR PPF 2278, Roosevelt Presidential Library.
9. Coyle to Brandeis, 6 February 1934, Brandeis Papers, University of Louisville.
10. Arthur Schlesinger, Jr., *The Crisis of the Old Order* (Boston, 1957), 189.
11. Felix Morley, *Washington Post*, 15 October 1934.
12. Ibid., 23 October 1934.
13. *New York Herald-Tribune*, 20 January 1935.
14. *New York Herald-Tribune*, 6 April 1935.

15. Frank Kent, reprinted in ibid., 11 April 1935.

16. Morley Journal, 3 March 1935.

17. Ibid., 28 March 1935.

18. Ibid., 27 May 1935.

19. Felix Morley, "A President Leaves His Party," *Washington Post*, 29 May 1935.

20. Morley Journal, 31 May 1935.

21. Ibid., 29 June 1935.

22. Felix Morley, *Washington Post*, 14 July 1935.

23. Ibid., 28 August 1935.

24. Felix Morley, *Washington Post*, 10 August 1935.

25. Ibid., 27 September 1935.

26. Morley Journal, 4 September 1935.

27. Ibid., 7 September 1935.

28. Ibid., 5 November 1935.

29. Ibid., 17 November 1935.

30. Ibid., 20 November 1935.

31. Ibid., 8 January 1936.

32. Felix Morley, *Washington Post*, 27 April 1936.

33. Ibid., 9 June 1936.

34. Morley Journal, 27 June 1936.

35. Ibid., 27 July 1936.

CHAPTER 6

1. Morley Journal, 22 September 1936.

2. *Washington Post*, 23 September 1936.

3. Ibid., 5 August 1936.

4. Ibid., 12 September 1936.

5. Morley Journal, 29 September 1936.

6. Ibid., 9 October 1936.

7. Ibid., 14 October 1936.

8. Burke, 2 February 1936.

9. Lower, 280–290.

10. Burke, 22 September 1936.

11. *The New Republic*, 11 November 1936.

12. Burke, 15 November 1936.

13. Mittell to Corcoran, 20 May 1937, Corcoran Papers.

14. Corcoran to Walling, 15 December 1937, ibid.

15. Corcoran to Mcgelever, 17 December 1937, ibid.

16. Corcoran to Gerald Voorhees, 17 December 1937, ibid.

17. David Cushman Coyle, *Why Pay Taxes?* (New York, 1937), passim.

18. Frankfurter to Bliven, 2 November 1936, Frankfurter Papers.

19. Frankfurter to Bliven, 20 November 1936, ibid.

20. Scidomann, 130.

21. *The New Republic*, 17 February 1937.

22. Ibid., 24 February 1937.

23. Ibid., 3 March 1937.

24. Ibid.
25. In FDR PPF, 1937.
26. Frankfurter to Laski, 11 May 1937, Frankfurter Papers.
27. Laski to LeHand, 18 May 1937, FDR, PPF.
28. Laski to Frankfurter, 3 August 1937, Frankfurter Papers.
29. *The New Republic*, 3 March 1937.
30. Seidemann, 133.
31. *New York Herald-Tribune*, 11 February 1937.
32. Ibid., 25 February 1937.
33. Quoted in *Wall Street Journal*, 28 April 1937.
34. Alpern, 108.
35. Ibid.
36. Ibid., 109.
37. *The Nation*, 13 February 1937.
38. Ibid., 13 March 1937.
39. Ibid.
40. Ibid., 20 February 1937.
41. Max Lerner, "Lippmann and the Court," in ibid, 27 February 1937, 230.
42. Alpern, 109–111.
43. *The Nation*, 27 March 1937.
44. Maurice Wertheim, "'The Nation' and the Court," in ibid., 10 April 1937, 399.
45. Heywood Broun, "Is There a Nation?" in ibid., 17 April 1937, 437.
46. Alpern, 112.
47. Ibid., 117.
48. Bliven to Frankfurter, 14 September 1937, Frankfurter Papers.
49. Alpern, 122.
50. Ibid., 125.
51. Coyle to Corcoran, n.d., but summer 1937, Corcoran Papers.

CHAPTER 7

1. Hapgood to Burton K. Wheeler, 9 March 1937, Norman Hapgood Papers, Library of Congress.
2. Martin Doudna, *Concerned About the Planet: The Reporter Magazine and American Liberalism* (Westport, Conn., 1977), 38–39.
3. Pinchot to members of Congress, 13 February 1937, Pinchot Papers.
4. Pinchot to Howard, 16 February 1937, ibid.
5. Pinchot to Hans Cohrssen, 18 February 1937, ibid.
6. Pinchot to Stephen Wise, 26 February 1937, ibid.
7. Pinchot to FDR, 26 April 1937, ibid.
8. James Truslow Adams to Edward A. Rumely, 25 May 1937, copy in ibid.
9. Wheeler to Pinchot, 28 May 1937, ibid.
10. Ekirch, 199.
11. Burke, 6 February 1937.
12. Ibid., 14 February 1937.
13. Ibid.
14. Ibid., 9 April 1937.

15. Ibid., 292.
16. Ibid., 26 March 1937.
17. Ibid., 16 April 1937.
18. Ibid., 7 May 1937.
19. Ibid., 29 May 1937; 5 June 1937.
20. Morley Journal, 5 February 1937.
21. Ibid., 4 March 1937.
22. Ibid.
23. Felix Morley, *Washington Post*, 9 March 1937.
24. Morley Journal, 13 March 1937.
25. *Washington Post*, 6 March 1937.
26. Morley Journal, 18 March 1937.
27. Ibid., 5 May 1937.
28. Bliven to FDR, 21 May 1937, Roosevelt Papers, PPF.
29. FDR to Bliven, 25 May 1937, ibid.
30. Ekirch, 204.
31. Corcoran Memoirs, "Pack" C/1.
32. Bruce Bliven, *The New Republic*, 14 July 1937.
33. Ibid., 25 August 1937.
34. Seidemann, 135.
35. Ibid.
36. Bliven to Malcom Cowley, 7 February 1937, Malcolm Cowley Papers, Newberry Library.
37. Bruce Bliven, "Twilight of Capitalism," *American Mercury*, September 1938, 86–87.
38. Walter Lippmann, *The Good Society* (New York, 1936), 3–4.
39. Ibid., 5.
40. Ibid., 8, 21.
41. Ibid., 49, 51, 52.
42. Ibid., 52.
43. Ibid., 103–104.
44. Ibid., 107.
45. Ibid., 108.
46. Ibid., 110, 123.
47. Ibid., 174–175.
48. Ibid., 236–237.
49. Ibid., 348.
50. Ibid., 365.

CHAPTER 8

1. *The New Republic*, 29 September 1937.
2. *The Nation*, 27 November 1937.
3. *New York Herald-Tribune*, 22 February 1934.
4. Laski to Frankfurter, 3 August 1937, Frankfurter Papers.
5. *North American Review* 244 (December 1937): 384.
6. Ekirch, 203–204.
7. *New York Herald-Tribune*, 19 October 1937.

8. Ibid., 21 October 1937.
9. Ibid., 4 January 1938.
10. Pinchot to Dorothy Thompson, 26 May 1937, Pinchot Papers.
11. Pinchot to Wheeler, 27 May 1937, ibid.
12. Pinchot to Howard, 1 June 1937, ibid.
13. Pinchot to Mrs. Alfred Hawes, 2 June 1937, ibid.
14. Pinchot to William Hard, 27 May 1937, ibid.
15. Pinchot to Max Eastman, 15 June 1937, ibid.
16. Pinchot to Howard, 16 June 1937, ibid.
17. Pinchot to George Parker, 28 June 1937, ibid.
18. Pinchot to Homer Bone, 16 July 1937, ibid.
19. Pinchot to Howard, 20 July 1937, ibid.
20. Pinchot to Hays Sulzberger, 22 July 1937, ibid.
21. Pinchot to Howard, 22 July 1937, ibid.
22. Pinchot to FDR, 26 July 1937, ibid.
23. Pinchot to Block, 9 August 1937, ibid.
24. Pinchot to Charles E. Merrill, 7 October 1937, ibid.
25. Pinchot to Eugene H. Briggs, 7 October 1937, ibid.
26. Lincoln Colcord to Pinchot, 2 November 1937, ibid.
27. Pinchot to Roy Howard, 26 November 1937, ibid.
28. Pinchot to Darwin J. Meserole, 8 December 1937, ibid.
29. Pinchot to Paul Block, 10 December 1937, ibid.
30. Pinchot to S. H. Evans, 29 December 1937, ibid.
31. Pinchot to John Leavell, 29 December 1937, ibid.
32. Pinchot to Samuel Pettengill, 5 January 1938, ibid.
33. Pinchot to Oswald Garrison Villard, 3 March 1938, ibid.
34. Pinchot to Robert Shriver, 21 April 1938, ibid.
35. McNary to George Putnam, 28 January 1938, McNary Papers.
36. Pinchot to Huntington Wilson, 2 May 1938, Pinchot Papers.
37. Pinchot to Howard, 14 May 1938, ibid.
38. Pinchot to FDR, 17 May 1938, ibid.
39. Pinchot to Richard Hurd, 17 June 1938, ibid.
40. Pinchot to Lewis, 3 September 1938, ibid.

CHAPTER 9

1. Burke, 12 June 1937.
2. Lower, 299.
3. Gary Dean Best, *Critical Press and the New Deal* (Westport, Conn., 1993), 138.
4. Burke, 17 July 1937.
5. Ibid., 24 July 1937.
6. Ibid., 1 August 1937.
7. Lower, 297.
8. Ibid., 299.
9. Burke, 19 February 1938.
10. Ibid., 16 April 1938.
11. Ibid., 26 February 1938.

12. Ibid., 26 March 1938.

13. Ibid., 10 April 1938.

14. Burke, 13 May 1938.

15. Ibid., 28 May 1938.

16. Morley Journal, 16 August 1937.

17. Ibid., 13 September 1937.

18. *Washington Post*, 14 October 1937.

19. Ibid., 11 November 1937.

20. Morley Journal, 31 March 1938.

21. Ibid., 8 April 1938.

22. Ibid., 31 August 1938.

23. Harold Laski, "Constitution under Strain," *Political Quarterly* 8 (October 1937): 507–516.

24. Walter Lippmann, *New York Herald-Tribune*, 12 March 1938.

25. Ibid., 19 April 1938.

26. Pinchot to Wesley Stout, 10 November 1938, Pinchot Papers.

27. Pinchot to Saul Haas, 14 November 1938, ibid.

28. Morley Journal, 13 September 1938.

29. Quoted in Lower, 304.

30. Ibid., 302.

31. Ibid.

32. Raymond Moley, *Newsweek*, 9 September 1940.

33. Lower, 328–329.

34. Burke, 19 January 1941.

35. Henry Hazlitt, *New York Times Book Review*, 8 January 1939.

36. Roosevelt Papers, PPF.

37. Laski to FDR, 5 January 1939, ibid.

38. FDR to Laski, 10 January 1939, ibid.

39. FDR to Laski, 31 January 1939, ibid.

40. Laski to FDR, 21 March 1939, ibid.

41. Laski to FDR, August 1939, ibid.

42. Laski to FDR, 3 September 1939, ibid.

43. Harold Laski, "America Revisited," *The New Republic*, 19 December 1939.

44. Harold Laski, "Public Opinion and the President," *Saturday Review of Literature*, 20 July 1940.

45. Ibid., 17 April 1937, 437. Raymond Morley, *Newsweek*, 9 September 1940.

EPILOGUE

1. Ekirch, 138.

2. Corcoran Memoirs, "Pack," C/1.

3. *New York Herald-Tribune*, 10 November 1938.

4. Corcoran Memoirs, "Pack," C/3.

5. *Time*, 12 November 1939, 21–22.

6. Schlesinger, *The Politics of Upheaval*, 174.

7. In Berle Papers, Roosevelt Presidential Library.

Bibliography

MANUSCRIPT COLLECTIONS AND ORAL HISTORY

Newton Baker Papers, Library of Congress
Charles Beard Papers, Library of Congress
Adolf A. Berle Papers, Franklin D. Roosevelt Presidential Library
Bruce Bliven Oral History, Columbia University
Louis Brandeis Papers, University of Louisville
Thomas G. Corcoran Papers and Memoirs, Library of Congress
Malcolm Cowley Papers, Newberry Library
Felix Frankfurter Papers, Library of Congress
Norman Hapgood Papers, Library of Congress
Harold Laski Papers, Syracuse University
Amos Pinchot Papers, Library of Congress
Charles McNary Papers, Library of Congress
Eugene Meyer Papers, Library of Congress
Henry Morgenthau Diary, Franklin D. Roosevelt Presidential Library
Felix Morley Papers and Journal, Hoover Presidential Library
John Callan O'Laughlin Papers, Library of Congress
Franklin Delano Roosevelt Papers, Franklin D. Roosevelt Presidential Library
Rexford Tugwell Papers, Franklin D. Roosevelt Presidential Library

BOOKS

Alpern, Sara. *Freda Kirchwey: A Woman of The Nation*. Cambridge, Mass., 1987.

Berman, Andrew. *We're in the Money*. New York, 1971.

Best, Gary Dean. *Nickel and Dime Decade*. Westport, Conn., 1991.

———. *Critical Press and the New Deal*. Westport, Conn., 1993.

Bliven, Bruce. *Five Million Words Later*. New York, 1970.

Burke, Robert E., ed. *Diary Letters of Hiram Johnson, 1917–1945*. New York, 1983.

Coyle, David Cushman. *The Irrepressible Conflict*. New York, 1932.

———. *Why Pay Taxes?* New York, 1937.

Croly, Herbert. *The Promise of American Life*. New York, 1909.

Doudna, Martin. *Concerned About the Planet: The Reporter Magazine and American Liberalism*. Westport, Conn., 1977.

Ekirch, Arthur. *Ideologies and Utopias*. Chicago, 1969.

Hamilton, Ian. *Writers in Hollywood*. New York, 1990.

Laski, Harold. *The Dangers of Obedience and Other Essays*. London, 1930.

———. *Democracy in Crisis*. New York, 1969. Reprint.

Lippincott, Isaac. *Sold Out*. New York, 1936.

Lippmann, Walter. *The Good Society*. New York, 1936.

Lower, Richard Coke. *A Bloc of One*. Stanford, Calif., 1993.

Lowi, Theodore J. *The End of Liberalism*. New York, 1979.

———. *The Crisis of the Old Order*. Boston, 1957.

Schlesinger, Arthur, Jr. *The Politics of Upheaval*. Boston, 1960.

Seidemann, David. *The New Republic*. New York, 1986.

Tweed, Thomas. *Gabriel Over the White House*. Garden City, N.Y., 1933.

Young, James P. *Reconsidering American Liberalism*. Boulder, Colo., 1996.

ARTICLES

Ascoli, Max. "Notes on Roosevelt's America." *Atlantic*, June 1934.

———. "Retreat from Liberalism." *The New Republic*, 10 April 1935, 249.

Bliven, Bruce. "Walter Lippmann and National Government." *The New Republic*, 23 September 1936.

———. "Twilight of Capitalism." *American Mercury*, September 1938, 86–87.

Broun, Heywood. "Is There a Nation?" *The Nation*, 17 April 1937.

Coyle, David Cushman. "Necessary Changes in Public Opinion in the New Social Order." *National Conference of Social Work*, 1933.

———. "Public Works, A New Industry." *Atlantic*, December 1933.

———. "Illusions Regarding Revolution." *Survey*, July 1934.

———. "Recovery and Finance." *Virginia Quarterly Review* 10 (October 1934).

Dandieu, Arnaud. "Harold Laski—Political Philosopher." *Living Age* 339 (November 1930): 267–270.

Elliot, William Yandell. "The Modern State: Karl Marx and Mr. Laski." *The Southern Review* 1 (1935): 209–223.

Greb, Gordon. "7 Million Words Later: An Interview with Bruce Bliven." *San Jose Studies* 2, no. 2.

Laski, Harold. "Roosevelt the Fighter." *Living Age* 343 (January 1933): 385–388.

———. "The Roosevelt Experiment." *Atlantic*, February 1934.

———. "Freedom in Danger." *Yale Review*, March 1934.

———. "The Challenge of Our Times." *American Scholar*, October 1939, 387–399.

Lerner, Max. "Lippmann and the Court." *The Nation*, 27 February 1937, 230.

McDonald, William. "Mr. Laski Takes the State Apart." *New York Times Book Review*, 24 March 1935.

Tugwell, Rexford. "The Principle of Planning and the Institution of Laissez Faire." *Supplement to the American Economic Review* 32 (March 1932).

PERIODICALS (SELECTED ISSUES)

Athens (Georgia) Daily Times
Atlanta Constitution
Literary Digest
Living Age
The Nation
The New Republic
Newsweek
New York Evening Post
New York Herald-Tribune
New York Times
New York World Telegram
North American Review
Omaha World Herald
Politica Quarterly
Redbook
Saturday Review of Literature
St. Louis Post-Dispatch
Time
Wall Street Journal
Washington Post

Index

Adams, James Truslow, 109
Agricultural Adjustment Act
  (AAA), 4, 6, 8, 9, 23, 32, 33, 64,
  66–67, 71, 72, 83, 93
American Association of Social
  Workers, 60
American Bar Association, 28
Ascoli, Max, 13–14, 32, 56–57, 107

Bankhead Bill, 28
Beard, Charles, 64
Berle, Adolf, 8, 12, 53
Black, Hugo, 115
Bliven, Bruce, 3, 7, 8, 10, 13, 16,
  17, 31, 32, 61, 64, 65, 94, 95,
  105, 113, 115, 143; background,
  11–12; and columnists, 114–115;
  American Mercury article, 115–
  116
Block, Paul, 132
Bone, Homer, 130
Borah, William, 31, 39, 68, 72

Brandeis, Louis, 2, 5, 7, 8, 9, 10,
  17, 32, 34, 41–42, 45, 46, 48, 49,
  59, 68, 78, 79, 82, 83, 86, 105,
  114, 123
Broun, Heywood, 102, 104
Burke, Edmund, 123

Cardozo, Benjamin, 61
Chase, Stuart, 100
Chavez, Dennis, 38–39
Chicago *Tribune*, 94–95
Cohen, Ben, 34
Colcord, Lincoln, 132
Colm, Gerhard, 143
Corcoran, Thomas, 4–5, 6, 13, 34,
  60, 78, 93–94, 98, 105, 114, 128,
  149
Couzens, James, 38
Coyle, David Cushman, 2, 9, 10,
  42, 65, 78–79, 80–82, 83, 93,
  105, 117, 123, 143; background,
  42–43; and Felix Frankfurter, 43;

Coyle, David Cushman (*continued*)
  The Irrepressible Conflict, 42–
  45; *National Conference of Social
  Work* article, 75–77; *Atlantic
  Monthly* article, 77–78; *Survey*
  article, 79–80; *Virginia Quar-
  terly Review* article, 79–80; *Why
  Pay Taxes?*, 93–94
Cravath, Paul, 67
Croly, Herbert, 4
Cutting, Bronson, 38–39
Douglas, Lewis, 87–88

Eastman, Max, 130
Eccles, Marriner, 66, 68, 69, 83, 113
Ekirch, Arthur, 7, 9, 113
Elliott, William, 55–56

Fairchild, Henry Pratt, 24
Farley, James, 60
Flanders, Ralph, 74
Frank, Jerome, 34
Frankfurter, Felix, 4, 7–8, 9, 11–
  12, 13, 17, 31, 32, 34, 41, 42–43,
  45, 48, 52, 55–7, 59, 60, 61, 62,
  70, 71, 74, 78, 91, 94, 95, 98,
  134, 151
Frazier–Lemke Act, 68, 85

Gabriel Over the White House, 14–
  17
Gannett, Frank, 69. 109
Gardner, Gilson, 22
Goldsborough Amendment, 67–68
Graham, Otis, 2

Harriman, Henry, 12
Hartz, Louis, 3
Haywood, William, 11
Hazlitt, Henry, 146–147
Hearst, William Randolph, 15–17,
  94, 95, 102
Holmes, John Hayes, 74
Hoover, Herbert, 11, 14, 21, 22, 37,
  38,60, 73, 92
Howard, Roy, 23, 73, 87, 108, 129,
  130, 131

Howe, Ben, 67
Humphrey, William E., 85

Ickes, Harold, 21, 32, 37, 73, 74, 92
Inflationists, 8

Johnson, Hiram, 10, 31, 37–40, 92–
  93, 110–111, 137–139, 145–146
Johnson, Hugh, 130

Kent, Frank, 32, 83–84, 95, 114
Keynes, John Maynard, 17–18, 21,
  115
Kirchwey, Freda, 3, 10, 19–20, 65,
  66, 100, 102, 104–105
Knox, John, 108

LaFollette, Robert, 31, 67
Landis, James, 61
Landon, Alfred, 61–62, 64, 65, 89
Laski, Harold, 3, 4, 8, 9, 10, 11, 31,
  42, 45, 46, 48–49, 52, 54, 57, 59,
  60, 61, 62, 91, 97, 98, 115, 123,
  125, 134, 141, 146–148, 149–150,
  151, 153–154; debates Keynes in
  Redbook, 18–19; *Democracy in
  Crisis*, 47–48; *Atlantic* article,
  50–51; *Yale Review* article, 51;
  American Scholar article, 51–52;
  Politica article, 52–53; debate
  with Berle, 53
Lawrence, David, 114
Lehman, Fritz, 143
Lend-Lease Act, 146
Lerner, Max, 31, 100, 101–102,
  113, 124–125
Lewis, John L., 92, 114, 130, 136
Lewis, Sinclair, 107
Lippincott, Isaac, 5
Lippmann, Walter, 1, 10, 14, 16, 31–
  34, 35, 36, 37, 48, 49, 62–64, 65,
  83–84, 98–99, 101–102, 114, 115,
  117–129, 140, 143–144; Johns
  Hopkins lecture, 99–100; *The
  Good Society*, 116–121, 122–127
Los Angeles Times, 95
Lower, Richard, 38

Lowi, Theodore J., 6–7

McFadden, Barnarr, 14
McNary, Charles, 40, 134
Meyer, Eugene, 27
Moley, Raymond, 8, 9, 12, 34, 145–
    146, 150
Morgenthau, Henry, 71
Morley, Felix, 10, 27–31, 83, 84–
    89, 91–92, 112–113, 139–141,
    144–145
Mumford, Lewis, 123

The Nation, 2, 3, 4, 10, 16, 17, 19–
    20, 31, 60, 65, 66, 100–101, 102–
    105, 124–125, 127, 134
National Industrial Recovery Act
    (NIRA), 4, 8, 9, 33, 66
National Unemployment League,
    133
Nevins, Allan, 127
Newark Ledger, 93–94
New Freedom, 3
New Nationalism, 3
The New Republic, 2, 3, 7, 10, 11,
    12, 13, 16, 17, 52, 61, 64, 65, 97,
    105, 123, 127
New York Herald-Tribune, 31, 65,
    94, 107
New York Post, 24, 94
Norris, George, 31, 37

Oliphant, Herman, 71
Omaha World Herald, 36
O'Mahoney, Joseph C., 113
Owen, Robert, 67

People's League for Economic
    Security, 68
Pepper, Claude, 139
Philadelphia Record, 94
Pinchot, Amos, 10, 20–25, 31–32,
    33, 49, 66–74, 107–110, 125–
    127, 129–136, 137, 144
Polity, 21, 22
Progressives for Roosevelt, 21, 31
Promise of American Life, 4

Public Ownership League, 67
Public Utilities Holding Act, 40

Reciprocal Tariff Act, 38
Reconstruction Finance Corpora-
    tion (RFC), 67
Redbook, 18
Reorganization Bill, 111
Richberg, Donald, 9
Roosevelt, Franklin Delano, 1, 2,
    3, 4, 5, 6, 8, 9, 12, 13, 14, 16, 17,
    18, 20, 21, 22, 21, 24, 27, 28, 29,
    30, 32, 33, 34, 35, 36, 37, 38, 39,
    40, 45, 48, 49, 50, 52, 59, 60, 62,
    63, 64, 65, 66, 67, 68, 69, 70, 71,
    72, 73, 74, 84, 85, 86, 87, 88, 89,
    92, 93, 95, 98, 99, 100, 101, 107,
    108, 109, 110, 111, 112, 113,
    115, 128, 129, 130, 131, 132,
    133, 134, 135, 136, 137, 138,
    139, 140, 141, 143, 144, 145,
    147, 148, 152
Roosevelt, Theodore, 5
Rousseau, Jean Jacques, 4

St. Louis Post Dispatch, 36
Schlesinger, Arthur, Jr., 45, 78, 79
Securities Act of 1933, 17, 28, 29
Seideman, David, 64, 95, 98
Seldes, George, 107
Shaw, Albert, 70
Smith, Al, 63
Social Security Act, 65, 88
Sokolsky, George, 114
Soule, George, 7–8, 12, 31, 61
Steffens, Lincoln, 11
Sullivan, Mark, 32, 34, 36, 114
Sulzberger, Arthur Hays, 131
Supreme Court, 3, 6, 7, 9, 36, 41,
    49, 54, 59, 63, 64, 68, 69, 72, 85,
    88, 95, 104, 105, 107–111, 112,
    113, 114, 115, 125, 132, 133,
    134, 138, 139, 142, 145
Swope, Gerard, 12

Thomas Amendment, 38
Thompson, Dorothy, 95, 129

Tugwell, Rexford, 5, 6, 8, 9, 12, 13, 34, 68, 71–72, 83, 87, 98, 151

Villard, Oswald Garrison, 32, 102–104, 134
Voorhees, Jerry, 94

Wages and Hours Bill, 135, 137–138
Wagner Act, 29, 40
Wallace, Henry A., 125
Washington Post, 27, 28, 29, 35, 83, 85, 88, 91, 112

Wells, H. G., 131
Wertheim, Maurice, 103–104
Wheeler, Burton K., 9, 104, 107, 110, 129
White, William Allen, 73, 84
Wilson, Edmund, 5, 46
Wirt, William, 28
Works Progress Administration (WPA), 60, 98
World Court, 39

Young, James, 2–3, 5

ABOUT THE AUTHOR

Gary Dean Best is Emeritus Professor of History at the University of Hawaii. His previous books include *Pride, Prejudice, and Politics* (Praeger, 1990), *FDR and the Bonus Marchers* (Praeger, 1992), and *The Nickel and Dime Decade* (Praeger, 1993).